Thai for Intermediate Learners

by
Benjawan Poomsan Becker
(เบญจวรรณ ภูมิแสน เบคเกอร์)

PAIBOON

PUBLISHING

ภาษาไทย

- 299 BAHT -

Thai for Intermediate Learners

Paiboon Poomsan Publishing
582 Amarinniwate Village 2
Sukhapiban Road 1, Bungkum
Bangkok 10230
THAILAND
☎ 662-509-8632
Fax 662-519-5437

Paiboon Publishing
PMB 192, 1442A Walnut Street
Berkeley, California USA 94709
☎ 1-510-848-7086
Fax 1-510-848-4521
E-Mail: paiboon@thailao.com
www.thailao.com

สำนักพิมพ์ไพบูลย์ภูมิแสน
582 หมู่บ้านอัมรินทร์นิเวศน์ 2
ถ. สุขาภิบาล 1 เขตบึงกุ่ม
ก.ท.ม. 10230
☎ 662-509-8632
โทรสาร 662-519-5437

E-Mail: paiboon@thailao.com
www.thailao.com

Edited by Craig Becker

ISBN 1-887521-01-1

Printed by Chulalongkorn University Printing House
Tel. 0-2218-3563 July 2010 [5309-204/2,000(2)]
http://www.cuprint.chula.ac.th

Introduction

THAI FOR INTERMEDIATE LEARNERS offers a natural continuation of THAI FOR BEGINNERS. The two books provide a basic foundation in reading, writing and speaking the Thai language.

THAI FOR INTERMEDIATE LEARNERS teaches vocabulary, sentence structure and conversation while keeping the student interested with cultural facts such as Thai holidays, the provinces of Thailand, Thai food and common Thai names.

Students using THAI FOR INTERMEDIATE LEARNERS are expected to possess basic reading and writing skills and a vocabulary of about 400 commonly used words. This can be learned by using THAI FOR BEGINNERS or by other means. THAI FOR INTERMEDIATE LEARNERS teaches more advanced sentence structure and vocabulary than THAI FOR BEGINNERS. Although students should avoid transliteration, new vocabulary words are presented in both transliteration and Thai script. Emphasis is placed on real life conversation and reading skills. Each chapter ends with a test of the new skills learned. The book concludes with English translations of all sentences and conversations used in the lessons.

After you learn to read and write Thai, you will prefer using the Thai alphabet to the English transliteration. In the long run, it will save you a great deal of time. Instead of learning only speaking and listening skills and remaining illiterate in Thai, you will be able to function in all four skill — listening, speaking, reading and writing. Since it uses a phonetic alphabet, reading and writing Thai reinforces the other skills.

Table of Contents

Guide to Pronunciation   7

Lesson 1   11
Directions; Thai place names, public holidays; provinces

Lesson 2   27
More directions; Bangkok place names

Lesson 3   43
Using "ให้"

Lesson 4   57
Using "การ" and "ความ"

Lesson 5   71
Using "ที่", "ว่า" and "ถูก"

Lesson 6   85
Using "ใจ", "ขี้" and "น่า"

Lesson 7   103
Thai names; food; desserts; English names used in Thai

Lesson 8   121
More about kinship terms, pronouns

Lesson 9   141
Using particles

Lesson 10   161
The twelve year cycle; words from English

English Translation   179

Test Answers   205

Guide to Pronunciation

Tones

Because Thai is a tonal language, its pronunciation presents new challenges for English speakers. If the tone is wrong, you will not be easily understood even if everything else is correct. Thai uses five tones. For example, to pronounce a rising tone, your voice starts at a low pitch and goes up (much like asking a question in English). The phonetic transliteration in this text book uses tone marks over the vowels to show the tone for each word. Note that the tone marks used for transliteration are different from those used in Thai script.

Tone Marks (Transliteration)

Tone	Tone symbol	Example
mid	*None*	maa
low	`	màa
falling	^	mâa
high	´	máa
rising	ˇ	mǎa

Vowels

Most Thai vowels have two versions, short and long. Short vowels are clipped and cut off at the end. Long ones are drawn out. This book shows short vowels with a single letter and long vowels with double letters ('a' for short; 'aa' for long).

The 'ʉ' has no comparable sound in English. Try saying 'u' while spreading your lips in as wide a smile as possible. If the sound you are making is similar to one you might have uttered after stepping on something disgusting, you are probably close!

Short & Long Vowels

a	*like a in Alaska*	fan - *teeth*
aa	*like a in father*	maa - *come*
i	*like i in tip*	sìp - *ten*
ii	*like ee in see*	sìi - *four*
u	*like oo in boot*	kun - *you*
uu	*like u in ruler*	sǔun - *zero*
ʉ	*like u in ruler, but with a smile*	nʉ̀ng - *one*
ʉʉ	*like ʉ but longer*	mʉʉ - *hand*
e	*like e in pet*	sèt - *finish*
ee	*like a in pale*	pleeng-*song*
ɛ	*like a in cat*	lɛ́ - *and*
ɛɛ	*like a in sad*	dɛɛng - *red*
ə	*like er in teacher without the r sound*	lə́ - *dirty*
əə	*like ə but longer*	jəə - *meet*
o	*like o in note*	jon - *poor*
oo	*like o in go*	joon -*robber*
ɔ	*like au in caught*	gɔ̀ - *island*
ɔɔ	*like aw in law*	nɔɔn - *sleep*

Complex Vowels

The following dipthongs are combinations of the above vowels.

ai	mâi - *not*		aai	saai - *sand*
ao	mao - *drunk*		aao	kâao - *rice*
ia	bia - *beer*		iao	nǐao - *sticky*
ua	dtua- *body*		uai	ruai - *rich*
ʉa	rʉa - *boat*		ʉai	nʉ̀ai - *tired*
ɔi	nɔ̀i - *little*		ɔɔi	kɔɔi - *wait*
ooi	dooi - *by*		əəi	nəəi - *butter*
ui	kui - *chat*		iu	hǐu - *hungry*
eo	reo - *fast*		eeo	eeo - *waist*
ɛo	tɛ̌o - *row*		ɛɛo	lɛ́ɛo - *already*

Consonants

b	as in *baby*	bin - *fly*
ch	as in *chin*	chûu - *name*
d	as in *doll*	duu - *look*
f	as in *fun*	fai - *fire*
g	as in *gold*	gin - *eat*
h	as in *honey*	hâa - *five*
j	as in *jet*	jèt - *seven*
k	as in *kiss*	kon - *person*
l	as in *love*	ling - *monkey*
m	as in *money*	mii - *have*
n	as in *need*	naa - *rice field*
p	as in *pretty*	pan - *thousand*
r	rolled like the Scottish *r*	rian - *study*
s	as in *sex*	sìi - *four*
t	as in *tender*	tam - *do*
w	as in *woman*	wan - *day*
y	as in *you*	yaa - *medicine*
ng	as in *ringing*	ngaan - *work*
dt	as in *stop*	dtaa - *eye*
bp	as in *spot*	bpai - *go*

The /dt/ sound lies between the /d/ and the /t/. Similarly, the /bp/ is between /b/ and /p/. (In linguistic terms, they are both unvoiced and unaspirated.) Unlike English, /ng/ frequently occurs at the beginning of words in Thai. Thai people often do not pronounce the /r/, replacing it with /l/ ('rian' will sound like 'lian'). When the /r/ is part of a consonant cluster, it is often dropped completely. ('kráp' will sound like 'káp'.)

Lesson 1
บทที่ ๑

บทที่ ๑

คำศัพท์   <u>Vocabulary</u>

ทาง	taang	way
ทิศทาง / ทิศ	tít-taang/tít	direction
ทางซ้าย (มือ)	taang-sáai (มือ)	on the left (hand side)
ทางขวา (มือ)	taang-kwǎa (มือ)	on the right (hand side)
ทางนี้	taang-níi	this way
ทางนั้น	taang-nán	that way
ทางโน้น	taang-nóon	that way (further)
ทางไหน	taang-nǎi	which way
ทางเข้า	taang-kâo	way in, entrance
ทางออก	taang-ɔ̀ɔk	way out, exit
ทางไปรษณีย์	taang-bprai-sà-nii	by mail
ทางอากาศ	taang-aa-gàat	by air
ทางไปรษณีย์อากาศ		by airmail
	taang-bprai-sà-nii-aa-gàat	
ทางทะเล	taang-tá-lee	by sea
ทางบก	taang-bòk	by land
ข้าง	kâang	side
ข้างซ้าย (มือ)	kâang-sáai (มือ)	left (hand) side
ข้างขวา (มือ)	kaang-kwǎa (มือ)	right (hand) side
ข้างหน้า	kâang-nâa	in the front
ข้างหลัง	kâang-lǎng	in the back
ข้างไหน	kâang-nǎi	which side, where
และ / กับ	lé/gàp	and

เกินไป/ไป	gəən-bpai/bpai	excessively, too
ไปด้วย	bpai-dûai	to go together
ภาค	pâak	region
เหนือ	nǔa	north
ใต้	dtâai	south
ตะวันออก	dtà-wan-ɔ̀ɔk	east
ตะวันตก	dtà-wan-dtòk	west
ตะวันออกเฉียงเหนือ		northeast
	dtà-wan-ɔ̀ɔk-chǐang-nǔa	
ตะวันออกเฉียงใต้		southeast
	dtà-wan-ɔ̀ɔk-chǐang-dtâai	
ตะวันตกเฉียงเหนือ		northwest
	dtà-wan-dtòk-chǐang-nǔa	
ตะวันตกเฉียงใต้		southwest
	dtà-wan-dtòk-chǐang-dtâai	
(ภาค) อีสาน	(pâak) ii-sǎan	the Northeast
จังหวัด	jang-wàt	province
อำเภอ	ampəə	district
อำเภอเมือง	ampəə-mɯang	central district
เขต	kèet	district (in Bangkok)
ตำบล	dtambon	subdistrict, ward
หมู่บ้าน	mùu-bâan	village
รัฐ	rát	state
สหรัฐ	sà-hà-rát	the United States
ต่างจังหวัด	dtàang-jang-wàt	other province
ต่างอำเภอ	dtàang-ampəə	other district
ต่างประเทศ	dtàang-bprà-têet	other/ foreign country
ประเพณี	bprà-pee-nii	custom, tradition

วัฒนธรรม wáttá-ná-tam — culture

เทศกาล/งาน têetsà-gaan/ngaan — festival

ทำบุญ tambun — to make merit

ทำนา tamnaa — to farm rice

อากาศ aa-gàat — weather

ฤดูร้อน
  rú-duu — season

ฤดูร้อน/หน้าร้อน
  rú-duu-rɔ́ɔn/nâa-rɔ́ɔn — hot season, summer

ฤดูฝน/หน้าฝน
  rú-duu-fǒn/nâa-fǒn — rainy season

ฤดูหนาว/หน้าหนาว
  rú-duu-nǎao/nâa-nǎao — cold season, winter

ฤดูใบไม้ผลิ
  rú-duu-bai-maái-plì — spring

ฤดูใบไม้ร่วง
  rú-duu-bai-maái-rûang — autumn

โอกาส
  oo-gàat — opportunity

แถวนั้น
  tɛ̌ɛo-nán — that area

จัด
  jàt — to arrange, to organize

มารับ/ไปรับ
  maa-ráp/pai-ráp — to pick someone up

เพราะว่า
  prɔ́-wâa — because

Note: There is no spring or autumn in Thailand.

Public Holidays in Thailand
วันหยุดในประเทศไทย

วันปีใหม่ wan bpii mài   New Year's Day

- A recent public holiday: December 31-January 1.

วันมาฆบูชา   wan maa-ká-buu-chaa   Makabucha Day

- Held on the full moon of the third lunar month to commemorate the preaching of the Buddha to 1250 enlightened monks who came to hear him without prior summons.

วันจักรี   wan jàk-grii   King Rama I Day

- Commemorating the founder of the Jakgri Dynasty, Rama I, on April 6.

วันสงกรานต์   wan sŏng-graan   Thai New Year's Day

- April 12-14, main event on the 13th. The time when Thai people sprinkle water on one another.

วันฉัตรมงคล wan chàtmong-kon   Coronation Day

- The King and the Queen commemorate their 1946 coronation on May 5.

วันพืชมงคล wan pûutmong-kon   Royal Ploughing Day

-To start the official rice planting season in the second week of May.

วันวิสาขบูชา wan wí-sǎa-kà-buu-chaa   Wisakabucha Day

- The full moon in the 6th lunar month, which is considered the date of the Buddha's birth, enlightment and passing away.

วันอาสาฬหบูชา   wan aa-săan-hà-buu-chaa   Asanhabucha Day

- Commemorates the first sermon preached by the Buddha on the full moon in mid July.

วันเข้าพรรษา   wan kâo-pansăa   Buddhist Lent

- The beginning of Buddhist Lent, which is the traditional time of year for young men to enter the monkhood for the rainy season. All monks stay in a single temple without leaving for three months starting from mid to late July.

วันแม่ wan mɛ̂ɛ   Mother's Day

- Also Queen's birthday on August 12.

วันปิยะ wan bpì-yá   Chulalongkorn Day

- Commemoration of King Rama V on October 23.

วันพ่อ wan pɔ̂ɔ   Father's Day

- Also King's birthday and Thailand's National Day.

Other Festivals Celebrated Nationwide (No Holidays)

วันออกพรรษา   wan ɔ̀ɔkpan-săa

- The End of Buddhist Lent Day - around October.

วันลอยกระทง   wan lɔɔi grà-tong   Loy Gratong Day

- On the full moon night in November. Small lotus-shaped baskets or boats made of banana leaves containing flowers, incense, candles and coins are floated on rivers, lakes and canals. The time for the Thai to throw away their sins into the water.

Note: Recently, Thai people celebrate Valentine's Day and Christmas, not for religious purposes, but for fun. Neither day is a public holiday.

The 76 Provinces of Thailand

1. กรุงเทพ (มหานคร)   grung-têep(má-hǎa-ná-kɔɔn), Bangkok
2. กระบี่   grà-bìi
3. กาญจนบุรี   gaanjà-ná-bù-rii
4. กาฬสินธุ์   gaa-lá-sǐn
5. กำแพงเพชร   gampɛɛng-pét
6. ขอนแก่น   kɔ̌n-gɛ̀n
7. จันทบุรี   jan-tá-bù-rii
8. ฉะเชิงเทรา   chà-chəəng-sao
9. ชลบุรี   chon-bù-rii
10. ชัยภูมิ   chai-yá-puum
11. เชียงใหม่   chiang-mài
12. เชียงราย   chiang-raai
13. ชุมพร   chumpɔɔn
14. ชัยนาท   chai-nâat
15. ตราด   dtràat
16. ตาก   dtàak
17. ตรัง   dtrang
18. นครราชสีมา   ná-kɔɔn-râat-chá-sǐi-maa
19. นครนายก   ná-kɔɔn-naa-yók
20. นครพนม   ná-kɔɔn-pá-nom
21. นครปฐม   ná-kɔɔn-bpà-tǒm
22. นครศรีธรรมราช   ná-kɔɔn-sǐi-tammá-râat
23. นครสวรรค์   ná-kɔɔn-sà-wǎn
24. นนทบุรี   nontá-bù-rii
25. นราธิวาส   ná-raa-tí-wâat
26. น่าน   nâan
27. บุรีรัมย์   bù-rii-ram
28. ปทุมธานี   bpà-tumtaa-nii
29. ปราจีนบุรี   bpraa-jiin-bù-rii
30. ประจวบคีรีขันธ์   bprà-jùap-kii-rii-kǎn
31. ปัตตานี   bpàt-dtaa-nii
32. พะเยา   pá-yao
33. แพร่   prɛ̂ɛ
34. พิจิตร   pí-jìt
35. พิษณุโลก   pít-sà-nú-lôok
36. เพชรบูรณ์   pétchá-buun
37. เพชรบุรี   pétchá-bù-rii, pét-bù-rii

38.	พังงา	pang-ngaa
39.	พัทลุง	páttá-lung
40.	ภูเก็ต	puu-gèt
41.	มุกดาหาร	múkdaa-hǎan
42.	มหาสารคาม	má-hǎa-sǎa-rá-kaam
43.	แม่ฮ่องสอน	mɛ̂ɛ-hɔ̂ng-sɔ̌ɔn
44.	ยโสธร	yá-sǒo-tɔɔn
45.	ยะลา	yá-laa
46.	ร้อยเอ็ด	rɔ́ɔi-èt
47.	ระนอง	rá-nɔɔng
48.	ระยอง	rá-yɔɔng
49.	ราชบุรี	râatchá-bù-rii, râatbù-rii
50.	ลพบุรี	lópbù-rii
51.	ลำปาง	lam-bpang
52.	ลำพูน	lam-puun
53.	เลย	ləəi
54.	ศรีสะเกษ	sǐi-sà-gèet
55.	สกลนคร	sà-gonná-kɔɔn
56.	สงขลา	sǒng-klǎa
57.	สตูล	sà-dtuun
58.	สมุทรปราการ	sà-mùt-bpraa-gaan
59.	สมุทรสงคราม	sà-mùtsǒng-kraam
60.	สมุทรสาคร	sà-mùtsǎa-kɔɔn
61.	สระแก้ว	sà-gɛ̂ɛo
62.	สระบุรี	sà-rà-bù-rii
63.	สิงห์บุรี	sǐng-bù-rii
64.	สุโขทัย	sù-kǒo-tai
65.	สุพรรณบุรี	sù-panbù-rii
66.	สุราษฎร์ธานี	sù-râattaa-nii
67.	สุรินทร์	sù-rin
68.	หนองคาย	nɔ̌ɔng-kaai
69.	หนองบัวลำภู	nɔ̌ɔng-bua-lampuu
70.	อยุธยา	à-yúttá-yaa
71.	อ่างทอง	àang-tɔɔng
72.	อุบลราชธานี	ù-bon-râat-chá-taa-nii
73.	อุทัยธานี	ù-tai-taa-nii
74.	อุดรธานี	ù-dɔɔntaa-nii
75.	อุตรดิตถ์	ùt-dtrà-rá-dìt
76.	อำนาจเจริญ	amnâatjà-rəən

ประโยค

1. มาทางนี้
   ไปทางนั้น

2. รถอยู่ทางซ้าย
   บ้านอยู่ทางขวา

3. โรงแรมอยู่ทางไหน — อยู่ทางขวามือ
   ร้านอาหารไทยอยู่ทางไหน — อยู่ทางโน้น

4. หนังสืออยู่ข้างขวา
   ปากกาอยู่ข้างซ้าย
   ธนาคารอยู่ข้างหน้า
   สนามบินอยู่ข้างหลัง

5. ดินสออยู่ข้างไหน — อยู่ข้างซ้ายมือ
   โรงเรียนอยู่ข้างไหน — อยู่ข้างขวา

6. ส่งจดหมายทางอากาศ
   มาทางเรือ

7. เผ็ดเกินไป
   อาหารไทยเผ็ดเกินไป
   คิดว่าอาหารไทยเผ็ดเกินไป

8. ประเทศไทยมีสี่ภาค ภาคเหนือ ภาคอีสาน
    ภาคกลาง และภาคใต้

9. คุณมาจากภาคไหน   – มาจากภาคเหนือ
    เขามาจากภาคไหน   – มาจากภาคอีสาน

10. ประเทศไทยมีเจ็ดสิบหกจังหวัด

11. คุณมาจากจังหวัดอะไร   – มาจากกรุงเทพ
    เขามาจากจังหวัดอะไร   – มาจากเชียงราย

12. กรุงเทพมีสามสิบแปดเขต
    ภูเก็ตมีสามอำเภอ

13. คุณอยู่อำเภออะไร   – ผมอยู่อำเภอเมือง

14. เมืองไทยมีสามฤดู ฤดูร้อน ฤดูฝน
    และฤดูหนาว

15. ญี่ปุ่นมีกี่ฤดู
    – มีสี่ฤดู ฤดูใบไม้ผลิ ฤดูร้อน ฤดูใบไม้ร่วง
    และฤดูหนาว

16. ดิฉันชอบประเพณีไทยมาก
    เขารักวัฒนธรรมไทย

17. วันนี้วันอะไร   – วันนี้วันสงกรานต์

18. คนไทยทำบุญวันปีใหม่

19. ที่เมืองไทยทำนาหน้าฝน

20. เราจะไปงานวันลอยกระทง

<u>บทสนทนา ๑</u>

สมชัยกับแมรี่

แมรี่: ขอโทษค่ะ ธนาคารอยู่ที่ไหนคะ
สมชัย: อยู่ทางซ้ายมือครับ
แมรี่: ขอบคุณค่ะ
สมชัย: ไม่เป็นไรครับ

<u>บทสนทนา ๒</u>

มาลีกับจอห์น

มาลี: คุณจอห์นมาจากประเทศอะไรคะ
จอห์น: ผมมาจากอเมริกา รัฐเนวาดาครับ
แล้วคุณมาลีมาจากจังหวัดอะไรครับ
มาลี: จากเชียงใหม่ค่ะ แต่มาทำงานที่กรุงเทพ
คุณจะอยู่เมืองไทยกี่วันคะ
จอห์น: ประมาณสองอาทิตย์ครับ จะกลับอเมริกาวันที่สิบห้า

บทสนทนา ๓

เล็กกับอากิโกะ

เล็ก: คุณชอบเมืองไทยไหมคะ
อากิโกะ: ชอบมากค่ะ ชอบคนไทย อาหารไทย
               แต่คิดว่าอากาศร้อนเกินไป
เล็ก: แต่ที่ภาคเหนือและ ภาคอีสานมีฤดูหนาวนะคะ
อากิโกะ: จริงหรือคะ ดิฉันยังไม่มีโอกาสไปแถวนั้นเลย

บทสนทนา ๔

กิติกับมาร์ค

มาร์ค: วันนี้วันสงกรานต์ คุณจะไปเที่ยวที่ไหนไหมครับ
กิติ:   คิดว่าจะไปวัด   เพราะว่าปีนี้ที่วัดจัดงานใหญ่
มาร์ค: ผมขอไปด้วยได้ไหมครับ
กิติ:   ได้ครับ งานสงกรานต์ที่วัดสนุกทุกปี
มาร์ค: คุณจะไปเมื่อไหร่ครับ
กิติ:   วันอาทิตย์   ประมาณเที่ยง
               แล้วผมจะมารับนะครับ

Test 1

Match the English words with the Thai words.

_____ 1. east	a.	ฤดูใบไม้ร่วง
_____ 2. district	b.	จังหวัด
_____ 3. rainy season	c.	ทำนา
_____ 4. south	d.	อากาศ
_____ 5. village	e.	ตำบล
_____ 6. west	f.	ฤดูใบไม้ผลิ
_____ 7. province	g.	ภาค
_____ 8. hot season	h.	ตะวันออก
_____ 9. north	i.	หมู่บ้าน
_____ 10. region	j.	ฤดูร้อน
_____ 11. to make merit	k.	ตะวันตก
_____ 12. weather	l.	ฤดูฝน
_____ 13. spring	m.	เหนือ
_____ 14. to farm rice	n.	ทำบุญ
_____ 15. side	o.	ข้าง
	p.	อำเภอ
	q.	ใต้
	r.	ฤดูหนาว

Translate the following into English.

1. โรงเรียนอยู่ทางนั้น

_____

2. ผมไม่ชอบฤดูร้อน

_____

3. วันนี้อากาศดี

_____

4. คนนี้มาจากภาคใต้

_____

5. ดิฉันจะไปขอนแก่นอาทิตย์หน้า

_____

Lesson 2

บทที่ ๒

บทที่ ๒

คำศัพท์	Vocabulary
เลี้ยว líao	turn
ซ้าย sáai	left
ขวา kwǎa	right
ซ้ายมือ sáai-mɯɯ	left hand side
ขวามือ kwǎa-mɯɯ	right hand side
แล้ว lέεo	then
ตรง/ที่ dtrong/tîi	at
ตรงนี้ dtrong-níi	overhere, right here
ตรงนั้น dtrong-nán	overthere, right there
ตรงไป/ตรง dtrong-bpai/dtrong	straight
ก่อน gɔ̀ɔn	before
หลัง lǎng	after
ข้างหน้า/หน้า kâang-nâa/nâa	in front of, ahead
ข้างหลัง/หลัง kâang-lǎng/lǎng	behind
ข้างใน kâang-nai	inside
ข้างนอก kâang-nɔ̂ɔk	outside
ข้างบน kâang-bon	upstairs, above
ข้างล่าง kâang-lâang	downstairs, below
ชั้นบน chán-bon	upstairs
ชั้นล่าง chán-lâang	downstairs
สี่แยก sìi-yɛ̂ɛk	four way intersection
สามแยก sǎamyɛ̂ɛk	three way intersection
ป้ายรถเมล์ bpâai-rótmee	bus stop

เงินทอน ngən-tɔɔn	change
ทอน/ทอนเงิน tɔɔn/tɔɔn-ngən	to give change
แลก lɛ̂ɛk	to exchange
จ่าย jàai	to pay
จอด/หยุด jɔ̀ɔt/yùt	to stop
มีแต่ mii-dtɛ̀ɛ	to have only ...
ใบ bai	slip or sheet of paper (e.g. notes, money, tickets)
ใบร้อย/ใบละร้อย bai-rɔ́ɔi/bai-lá-rɔ́ɔi	one hundred bill
พัก pák	to stay, to rest
ถึง/ไปถึง/มาถึง tŭng/bpai-tŭng/maa-tŭng	to arrive
รับ ráp	to receive
ส่ง sòng	to send
ไปส่ง/มาส่ง bpai-sòng/maa-sòng	to see someone off
ซื้อของ/ชอปปิ้ง súʉ-kɔ̌ɔng/chɔ́ɔp-bpîng	to shop
สาธารณะ sǎa-taa-rá-ná	public
ห้องน้ำสาธารณะ hɔ̂ng-náam-sǎa-taa-rá-ná	public restroom
โทรศัพท์สาธารณะ too-rá-sàp-sǎa-taa-rá-ná	public telephone
สวนสาธารณะ sǔan-sǎa-taa-rá-ná	park
ปั๊มน้ำมัน bpám-náamman	gas station
ห้างสรรพสินค้า hâang-sàppá-sǐnkáa	department store
พิพิธภัณฑ์ pí-pít-tá-pan	museum

โรงพยาบาล roong-pá-yaa-baan	hospital
สถานทูต sà-tǎan-tûut	embassy
กระทรวง grà-suang	ministry
สถานี sà-tǎa-nii	station
สถานีวิทยุ sà-tǎa-nii-wíttá-yút	radio station
สถานีโทรทัศน์ sà-tǎa-nii-too-rá-tát	T.V. station
สถานีตำรวจ sà-tǎa-nii-dtamrùat	police station
สถานีดับเพลิง sà-tǎa-nii-dàpplaang	fire station
สถานีรถไฟ sà-tǎa-nii-rótfai	railway station
ขนส่ง kǒnsòng	bus terminal
ท่า/ท่าเรือ tâa/tâa-rɰa	port
เกาะ gɔ̀	island
ชายหาด chaai-hàat	beach
ซอย sɔɔi	lane, alley, Soi
คลอง klɔɔng	canal
อ่าว àao	gulf, bay
มหาสมุทร má-hǎa-sà-mùt	ocean
ทวีป tá-wîip	continent
เดี๋ยว dǐao	in a moment
โชคดี/โชคดีนะ chookdii/chookdii-ná	Good luck!

Places in Bangkok

โรงแรม **Hotels**

โรงแรมแอพอร์ต	roong-rɛɛm ɛɛ-pɔ̀ɔt	Airport Hotel
โรงแรมเอเชีย	roong-rɛɛm ee-chia	Asia Hotel
โรงแรมฮิลตัน	roong-rɛɛm hin-dtân	Hilton Hotel
โรงแรมมนเทียร	roong-rɛɛm montian	Montien Hotel
โรงแรมแม่น้ำ	roong-rɛɛm mɛ̂ɛ-náam	The Menam Hotel
โรงแรมแอมบาสเดอร์	roong-rɛɛm ɛmbá-sà-dɔ̂ə	Ambassador Hotel
โรงแรมดุสิตธานี	roong-rɛɛm dù-sìttaa-nii	Dusit Thani Hotel
โรงแรมเซนทรัลพลาซา	roong-rɛɛm sentrânplaa-sâa	Central Plaza Hotel
โรงแรมอิมพาลา	roong-rɛɛm impaa-lâa	Impala Hotel
โรงแรมอิมพีเรียล	roong-rɛɛm impii-rîan	Imperial Hotel
โรงแรมแมนฮัตตัน	roong-rɛɛm mɛɛnhát-dtân	Hotel Manhattan
โรงแรมแมนดาริน	roong-rɛɛm mɛɛndaa-rin	Mandarin Hotel
โรงแรมโอเรียนเต็ล	roong-rɛɛm ɔɔ-rian-dten	The Oriental Hotel
โรงแรมรามาทาวเวอร์	roong-rɛɛm raa-maa-taao-wɔ̂ə	Rama Tower
โรงแรมเชอราตัน	roong-rɛɛm chəə-raa-dtân	Royal Orchid Sheraton
โรงแรมรอยัลริเวอร์	roong-rɛɛm rɔɔ-yân-rí-wɔ̂ə	The Royal River

โรงแรมแชงกรีลา   Shangri-La Hotel
  roong-rɛɛm chɛng-grii-lâa
โรงแรมสีลมพลาซา   Silom Plaza
  roong-rɛɛm sǐi-lomplaa-sâa

ถนน Streets

ถนนเจริญกรุง   tà-nǒn jà-roen-grung   Charoen Krung

ถนนพหลโยธิน   tà-nǒn pá-hǒn-yoo-tin   Phahonyothin

ถนนพญาไท   tà-nǒn pá-yaa-tai   Phayathai

ถนนเพชรบุรี   tà-nǒn pétbù-rii   Phetburi

ถนนเพชรเกษม   tà-nǒn pétgà-sěem   Phetkasem

ถนนเพลินจิต   tà-nǒn pləənjìt   Ploenchit

ถนนพระราม ๑   tà-nǒn prá-raam nùng   Rama I

ถนนพระราม ๖   tà-nǒn prá-raam hòk   Rama VI

ถนนสาธรเหนือ   tà-nǒn sǎa-tɔɔn-nǔa   Sathon Nuea

ถนนสาธรใต้   tà-nǒn sǎa-tɔɔn-dtâai   Sathon Tai

ถนนสีลม   tà-nǒn sǐi-lom   Silom

ถนนสี่พระยา   tà-nǒn sìi-prá-yaa   Si Phaya

ถนนสุขุมวิท   tà-nǒn sù-kǔmwít   Sukhumvit

ถนนสุรวงศ์   tà-nǒn sù-rá-wong   Surawong

ถนนวิทย   tà-nǒn wíttá-yú   Wireless

ถนนวิภาวดีรังสิต   Wipawadirangsit
  tà-nǒn wí-paa-wá-dii-rang-sìt

ถนนเพชรบุรีตัดใหม่   New Phetburi
  tà-nǒn pétbù-rii-dtàtmài

ถนนรัชดาภิเษก   Ratchadapisek
  tà-nǒn rátchá-daa-pí-sèek

วัด **Temples**

วัดอรุณ wát à-run	Wat Arun
วัดเบญจมบพิตร wát benjà-má-bɔɔ-pít	Wat Benchamabophit
วัดบวรนิเวศน์ wát bɔɔ-wɔɔnní-wêet	Wat Bowonniwet
วัดมหาธาตุ wát má-hǎa-tâat	Wat Mahathat
วัดโพธิ์ wát poo	Wat Pho
วัดพระแก้ว wát prá-gɛ̂ɛo	Wat Phra Kaew
วัดระฆัง wát rá-kang	Wat Rakang
วัดสระเกษ wát sà-gèet	Wat Saket
วัดสุทัศน์ wát sù-tát	Wat Suthat
วัดไตรมิตร wát dtrai-mít	Wat Traimit

ธนาคาร **Banks**

ธนาคารกรุงเทพ tá-naa-kaan grung-têep	Bangkok Bank
ธนาคารไทยทนุ tá-naa-kaan tai-tá-nú	Thai Danu Bank
ธนาคารกรุงไทย tá-naa-kaan grung-tai	Krung Thai Bank
ธนาคารศรีอยุธยา tá-naa-kaan sǐi-à-yúttá-yaa	Bangkok of Ayudhya
ธนาคารแห่งประเทศไทย tá-naa-kaan hὲng bprà-têet-tai	Bank of Thailand
ธนาคารกสิกรไทย tá-naa-kaan gà-sì-gɔɔn-tai	Thai Farmers Bank
ธนาคารไทยพาณิชย์ tá-naa-kaan tai-paa-nít	Siam Commercial Bank
ธนาคารทหารไทย tá-naa-kaan tá-hǎan-tai	Thai Military Bank

กระทรวง **Ministries**

กระทรวงเกษตรและสหกรณ์
  grà-suang gà-sèet lé sà-hà-gɔɔn

Ministry of Agriculture and
Cooperatives

กระทรวงพาณิชย์
  grà-suang paa-nít

Ministry of Commerce

กระทรวงคมนาคม
  grà-suang ká-má-naa-kom

Ministry of Communications

กระทรวงกลาโหม
  grà-suang gà-laa-hŏom

Ministry of Defense

กระทรวงศึกษาธิการ
  grà-suang sùksǎa-tí-gaan

Ministry of Education

กระทรวงการคลัง
  grà-suang gaanklang

Ministry of Finance

กระทรวงต่างประเทศ
  grà-suang dtàang-bprà-têet

Ministry of Foreign Affairs

กระทรวงอุตสาหกรรม
  grà-suang ùtsǎa-hà-gam

Ministry of Industry

กระทรวงมหาดไทย
  grà-suang má-hàattai

Ministry of Interior

กระทรวงยุติธรรม
  grà-suang yút-dtì-tam

Ministry of Justice

กระทรวงสาธารณสุข
  grà-suang sǎa-taa-rá-ná-sùk

Ministry of Public Health

กระทรวงวิทยาศาสตร์ เทคโนโลยี และพลังงาน
  grà-suang wíttá-yaa-sàat téknoo-
  loo-yîi lé pá-lang-ngaan

Ministry of Science, Technology
and Energy

สวนสาธารณะ **Parks**

สวนหลวง ร. ๙ sǔanlǔang rɔɔ-gâao	Rama IX Royal Park
สวนลุม (พินี) sǔanlum(pí-nii)	Lumphini Park
สวนจัตุจักร suanjà-dtù-jàk	Chatuchak Park

พิพิธพัณฑ์ **Museum**

พิพิธพัณฑ์สถานแห่งชาติ pí-pít-tá-pan sà-tǎanhèng-châat	National Museum

<u>ประโยค</u>

1. โรงแรมดุสิตอยู่ทางซ้ายมือ

2. ตรงไปแล้วเลี้ยวขวา

3. เลี้ยวขวาก่อนแล้วเลี้ยวซ้าย

4. สถานีรถไฟอยู่ข้างหน้า

5. ข้างนอกอากาศร้อนมาก

6. ผมอยู่ข้างบน

7. ตรงไปข้างหน้า

8. ป้ายรถเมล์อยู่ตรงสี่แยก

9. จอดตรงนี้

10. มีแต่ใบร้อย มีเงินทอนไหม

11. ไม่มีเงินทอน

12. ผมจะไปถึงเมืองไทยพรุ่งนี้

13. จะไปรับเพื่อนที่สนามบิน

14. เขาไปซื้อของที่ห้าง (สรรพสินค้า)

15. เรานั่งแท็กซี่ไปสถานีรถไฟ

16. สถานทูตอเมริกาอยู่ถนนวิทยุ

17. ผมทำงานที่กระทรวงต่างประเทศ

18. มารับแฟนที่ขนส่ง

19. ที่กรุงเทพไม่ค่อยมีโทรศัพท์สาธารณะ

20. อยากไปเที่ยววัดพระแก้ว

บทสนทนา ๑

โทนี่กับคนขับแท็กซี่

คนขับแท็กซี่: จะไปไหนครับ

โทนี่:   ไปโรงแรมสุขุมวิทคราวน์

คนขับแท็กซี่: อยู่ซอยอะไรครับ

โทนี่:   สุขุมวิท ซอยแปด   ....
            เลี้ยวซ้าย จอดตรงนี้ .... เท่าไหร่ครับ

คนขับแท็กซี่: ห้าสิบบาทครับ

โทนี่:   ผมมีแต่ใบร้อย มีทอนไหม

คนขับแท็กซี่: ไม่มี เดี๋ยวผมจะไปแลกที่ร้านอาหารนะครับ

โทนี่:   ไม่เป็นไร ไม่ต้องทอนก็ได้

คนขับแท็กซี่: ขอบคุณครับ โชคดีนะ

บทสนทนา ๒

น้อยกับเดวิด

น้อย: คุณเดวิดจะกลับอเมริกาเมื่อไหร่ครับ

เดวิด: อีกสองวันครับ

น้อย: ผมอยากไปส่งคุณ คุณจะไปสนามบินกี่โมงครับ

เดวิด: ผมจะไปถึงสนามบินตอนสามทุ่ม เครื่องบินออกห้าทุ่ม

น้อย: โอเค แล้วเจอกันที่สนามบินตอนสามทุ่มนะครับ

<u>บทสนทนา ๓</u>

ทอมกับแดง

ทอม: ขอโทษครับ สถานทูตมาเลเซียอยู่ที่ไหนครับ

แดง: เดินตรงไป เลี้ยวซ้ายที่สี่แยกข้างหน้า
        แล้วเลี้ยวขวา   สถานทูตอยู่ทางขวามือครับ

ทอม: ขอบคุณมากครับ

แดง: ไม่เป็นไรครับ

Test 2

Match the English words with the Thai words.

_____ 1. bus stop	a.	โรงพยาบาล
_____ 2. intersection	b.	ข้างนอก
_____ 3. museum	c.	ซ้ายมือ
_____ 4. embassy	d.	สถานีรถไฟ
_____ 5. to see someone off	e.	ข้างบน
_____ 6. hospital	f.	ไปรับ
_____ 7. upstairs	g.	สาธารณะ
_____ 8. to give change	h.	ข้างใน
_____ 9. public	i.	จอด
_____ 10. to stop	j.	ข้างล่าง
_____ 11. downstairs	k.	สี่แยก
_____ 12. inside	l.	ไปส่ง
_____ 13. right hand side	m.	ขวามือ
_____ 14. railway station	n.	พิพิธภัณฑ์
_____ 15. to receive	o.	ทอนเงิน
	p.	รับ
	q.	ป้ายรถเมล์
	r.	สถานทูต

Translate the following into English.

1. คุณจะมาถึงเมืองไทยกี่โมง   - บ่ายสามโมง

_____

2. คุณจะพักที่ไหน   - ที่โรงแรมแม่น้ำ

_____

3. จะไปไหน   - จะไปช้อปปิ้ง

_____

4. สถานีตำรวจอยู่ที่ไหน   - เลี้ยวซ้ายแล้วตรงไป

_____

5. อยากไปเที่ยวที่ไหน   - อยากไปสวนลุม

_____

Lesson 3
บทที่ ๓

บทที่ ๓

คำศัพท์		Vocabulary
ให้	hâi	to give
ยืม/ขอยืม	yɯɯm/kɔ̌ɔ-yɯɯm	to borrow
ให้ยืม	hâi-yɯɯm	to lend
เช่า	châo	to rent from
ให้เช่า	hâi-châo	to rent to
ให้กำลังใจ	hâi-gamlang-jai	to encourage
ให้ได้	hâi-dâai	by all means
แก้	gɛ̂ɛ	to correct, to solve
เรียก	rîak	to call
ช่วย	chûai	to help
สัมภาษณ์	sǎmpâat	to interview
สัญญา	sǎn-yaa	to promise
ถ่ายรูป/ถ่าย	tàai-rûup/tàai	to take a picture
เปิด	bpɔ̀ɔt	to open, to turn on
ปิด	bpìt	to close, to turn off
เช็ด/ถู	chét/tǔu	to wipe
บริการ	bɔɔ-rí-gaan	to service, service
ส่ง	song	to send
ได้รับ/รับ	dâi-ráp/ráp	to receive
เอา	ao	to get, to want something
กับ/แก่	gàp/gɛ̀ɛ	to (somebody)
ที่อยู่	tîi-yùu	address
บ้านเลขที่	bâanlêektîi	address number

เบอร์โทร (ศัพท์)	bəə-too (rá-sàp)	telephone number
รหัสไปรษณีย์	rá-hàt-bprai-sà-nii	zip code
วันเกิด	wan gəət	birthday
ของขวัญ	kɔ̌ɔng-kwǎn	present, gift
หน้าต่าง	nâa-dtàang	window
ประตู	bprà-dtuu	door
ไฟ	fai	light
พัดลม	pátlom	fan
บัญชี	ban-chii	(bank) account
ความรู้	kwaamrúu	knowledge
การบ้าน	gaanbâan	homework
กรุณา/โปรด	gà-rú-naa/bpròot	please

How to Use ให้

ให้ by itself usually means 'to give'. However, it has many functions. The meaning of ให้ changes according to its position and the context. The following are common usages of ให้ :

1. subject + ให้ + direct object + (กับ) + indirect object
   = to give something to someone

      e.g.   เขาให้หนังสือ (กับ) ผม   He gives me a book.

             ผมให้เงินคุณ   I give you money.

2. subject + do something + ให้ + (กับ) + indirect object
   = to do something for somebody

      e.g.   เขาสอนภาษาไทยให้ผม He teaches me Thai.

             ผมทำงานให้คุณ   I work for you.

3. subject + ให้ + indirect object + do something
   = to make or have someone do something

      e.g.   เขาให้ผมสอนภาษาไทย He has me teach him Thai.

             ผมให้คุณทำงาน   I make you work./ I have
                                         you work.

4. subject + อยาก + ให้ + indirect object + verb
   = to want someone do something

      e.g.   เขาอยากให้ผมสอนภาษาไทย   He wants me to
                                        teach him Thai.

             ผมอยากให้คุณทำงาน   I want you to work.

5. subject + จะ + ให้ + object + do something
    = will make or have someone do something

    e.g.   เขาจะให้ผมสอนภาษาไทย   He will have me teach
                                    him Thai.
           ผมจะให้คุณทำงาน   I will make you work./
                                    I will have you work.

6. บอก + ให้ + object + do something   or
    บอก + object + ให้ + do something
    = to introduce an indirect command

    e.g.   บอกให้เขามาที่นี่   Tell him to come here.
           บอกเขาให้ทำงาน   Tell him to work.

7. subject + จะ + do something + ให้ + เอาไหม
    = to offer to do something for somebody

    e.g.   ผมจะสอนภาษาไทยให้ เอาไหม
           Do you want me to teach you Thai?

8. ให้ + adjective = adverb
    e.g.   ให้ชัด   clearly
           พูดให้ชัด   Speak clearly.

9. ให้ + หน่อย or ด้วย
        Use this combination at the end of the sentence to ask
    someone to do something for you in a nice and soft way. This
    phrase usually comes with the verb ช่วย or กรุณา.

    e.g.   ช่วยรับโทรศัพท์ให้ด้วย   Please answer the phone
                                    for me.
           ช่วยเปิดประตูให้หน่อย   Please open the door for me.

ประโยค

1. ใครให้การบ้านนักเรียน
   - ครูให้การบ้านนักเรียน
   คุณให้ของขวัญกับใคร
   - ผมให้ของขวัญกับแฟน

2. ใครสอนภาษาไทยให้คุณ
   - เขาสอนภาษาไทยให้ผม
   คุณสอนภาษาไทยให้ใคร
   - ผมสอนภาษาไทยให้เขา

3. ใครให้คุณไป   - เขาให้ผมไป
   คุณให้ใครไป   - ผมให้เขาไป

4. ใครอยากให้คุณไป   - เขาอยากให้ผมไป
   คุณอยากให้ใครไป   - ผมอยากให้เขาไป

5. ใครจะให้คุณไป   - เขาจะให้ผมไป
   คุณจะให้ใครไป   - ผมจะให้เขาไป

6. ผมจะถ่ายรูปให้ เอาไหม
   เราจะเขียนจดหมายให้ เอาไหม

7. เช็ดให้สะอาด
แก้ให้ถูก
กรุณาเขียนให้สวย

8. ช่วยปิดไฟให้ด้วย
ช่วยเรียกแท็กซี่ให้หน่อย
กรุณาเปิดพัดลมให้ด้วย

9. เราเช่าบ้านที่อเมริกา

10. ที่นี่มีบ้านให้เช่า

11. เขายืมเงินผม
ผมให้เขายืมเงิน

12. ดิฉันให้กำลังใจกับเพื่อน

13. มาให้ได้
เราจะไปเมืองไทยให้ได้

14. ผมสัมภาษณ์อาจารย์
ผมให้สัมภาษณ์กับทีวี

15. เขาสัญญากับดิฉัน = เขาให้สัญญากับดิฉัน

16. เรามีบริการดี = เราให้บริการดี

17. เขาไปส่งจดหมายให้ผม

18. ดิฉันได้รับของขวัญวันเกิด

19. เมื่อวานนี้ผมเปิดบัญชีที่ธนาคาร

20. คุณช่วยผมทำอาหาร

บทสนทนา ๑

สุดากับทิม

สุดา: คุณทิมพูดภาษาไทยเก่งมากเลย
ทิม: ยังไม่ค่อยเก่งครับ ฟังไม่ค่อยได้
สุดา: ใครสอนภาษาไทยให้คุณคะ
ทิม: อาจารย์คนไทยที่อเมริกาสอนให้ผมครับ
สุดา: อ่านเขียนได้ไหมคะ
ทิม: ได้นิดหน่อย อ่านช้าๆได้
　　　คุณสอนภาษาไทยให้ผมได้ไหมครับ
สุดา: ดิฉันอยากจะสอนให้คุณค่ะ แต่ไม่มีเวลา
　　　จะบอกเพื่อนให้นะคะ
ทิม: ขอบคุณครับ ผมอยากอ่านภาษาไทยให้เก่งๆ

บทสนทนา ๒

แอนกับเสรี

แอน: เบอร์โทรที่ทำงานของคุณเบอร์อะไรคะ
เสรี: เบอร์ 726-5921
แอน: ขอเบอร์โทรที่บ้านคุณด้วยค่ะ
เสรี: เบอร์ 654-0987

บทสนทนา ๓

เจนกับมาลี

เจน: คุณให้ที่อยู่กับดิฉันหรือยังค่ะ

มาลี:   ยังค่ะ

เจน: ช่วยบอกบ้านเลขที่ของคุณด้วยค่ะ

มาลี:   บ้านเลขที่ 390 ถนนดำเนิน อำเภอเมือง
          จังหวัดอุบล

เจน: คุณทราบรหัสไปรษณีย์ไหมคะ

มาลี:   34000 ค่ะ

เจน: ขอบคุณมากค่ะ

Test 3

Match the English words with the Thai words.

_____	1. light	a.	ยืม
_____	2. to send	b.	เรียก
_____	3. to borrow	c.	ปิด
_____	4. to turn on	d.	ช่วย
_____	5. window	e.	วันเกิด
_____	6. homework	f.	บริการ
_____	7. fan	g.	ไฟ
_____	8. to receive	h.	หน้าต่าง
_____	9. door	i.	ความรู้
_____	10. service	j.	บัญชี
_____	11. knowledge	k.	ของขวัญ
_____	12. account	l.	เปิด
_____	13. present	m.	รับ
_____	14. to take a picture	n.	ประตู
_____	15. to turn off	o.	ถ่ายรูป
		p.	การบ้าน
		q.	พัดลม
		r.	ส่ง

Translate the following into English.

1.   ไม่อยากให้คุณรู้

_____

2.   ช่วยทำอาหารไทยให้ด้วย

_____

3.   วันนี้เปิดบริการตอนเที่ยง

_____

4.   ผมอยากขอยืมเงินจากคุณ

_____

5.   อาจารย์ให้ความรู้กับนักเรียน

_____

Lesson 4
บทที่ ๔

บทที่ ๔

คำศัพท์	Vocabulary
การ gaan	work, matter, affair
ทหาร tá-hǎan	soldier
การทหาร gaantá-hǎan	military affairs
แพทย์ pêet	doctor
การแพทย์ gaanpêet	medicine, medical affairs
ป่าไม้ bpàa-máai	forest
การป่าไม้ gaan-bpàa-máai	forestry
ใช้ chái	to use
การใช้ gaanchái	usage
รักษา ráksǎa	to cure
การรักษา gaanráksǎa	remedy
จัดการ jàtgaan	to manage
การจัดการ gaanjàtgaan	management
ผู้จัดการ pûu-jàtgaan	manager
ตรวจ dtrùat	to examine, to inspect
การตรวจ gaan-dtrùat	examination, inspection
ศึกษา sùksǎa	to learn
การศึกษา gaansùksǎa	education
ความ kwaam	substance, matter
รัก rák	to love
ความรัก kwaamrák	love
รู้สึก rúu-sùk	to feel
ความรู้สึก kwaamrúu-sùk	feeling

หวัง wǎng	to hope
ความหวัง kwaamwǎng	hope
พยายาม pá-yaa-yaam	to try
ความพยายาม kwaampá-yaa-yaam	effort
สำเร็จ sǎmrèt	to succeed
ความสำเร็จ kwaamsǎmrèt	success
ตื่นเต้น dtùun-dtên	to be excited
ความตื่นเต้น kwaam-dtùun-dtên	excitement
ยากจน yâakjon	to be hard up, poor
ความยากจน kwaam-yâakjon	poverty
ยุติธรรม yú-dtì-tam	fair
ความยุติธรรม kwaam-yú-dtì-tam	justice
ยาว yaao	long
ความยาว kwaam-yaao	length
กว้าง gwâang	wide
ความกว้าง kwaam-gwâang	width
เร็ว reo	fast
ความเร็ว kwaam-reo	speed
สำคัญ sǎmkan	important
ความสำคัญ kwaamsǎmkan	importance
เศรษฐกิจ sèettà-gìt	economy
ปัญหา bpan-hǎa	problem
กฎหมาย gòtmǎai	law
ชาวต่างประเทศ	foreigner
chaao-dtàang-bprà-têet	

นิ้ว níu	inch
วา waa	"waa"- 2 meters
ไมล์ maai	mile
เมตร mêet	meter
กิโล (เมตร) gì-loo (mêet)	kilometer
ตารางวา dtaa-raang-waa	4 square meters
งาน ngaan	400 square meters
ไร่ râi	1600 square meters
ควร kwuan	should
ต้อง dtɔ̂ng	must
อาจจะ àat-jà	may
บางที baang-tii	maybe, perhaps
กล้า glâa	dare
ก็ได้ gɔ̂ɔ-dâai	(it) is all right (to)
ดีขึ้น dii-kûn	better
รัฐบาล rátta-baan	government
หนัก nàk	hard, difficult, heavy
ระยะ ráyá	period (time)
พา paa	to take someone to somewhere
บ้าง/มั่ง bâang/mâng	some, somehow

Note: When บ้าง or มั่ง occurs at the end of a question, it suggests that more than one item is expected to be mentioned in the answer.

e.g. คุณชอบสัตว์อะไรบ้าง	What animals do you like?
คุณอยากกินอะไรมั่ง	What do you want to eat?

How to Use การ

1. การ means work, affair or matter.

    e.g.   ในการนี้   in this matter

         เป็นการยาก   with difficulty

2. It is a prefix placed before nouns to form noun derivatives
   meaning "matters of ....".

    e.g.   การเมือง   politics (affairs of the state)

         การศึกษา   education

3. It is a prefix placed before active verbs to form noun
   derivatives signifying "act of (doing) ....".

    e.g.   การบิน   flying, aviation

         การช่วยเหลือ   assistance

4. It is a suffix used in compounds of Sanskrit origin.

    e.g.   กรรมการ   committee

         กิจการ   activity, business

         โครงการ   plan, project

How to Use ความ

1. ความ means the substance, the sense, the gist (of a matter, an account, etc.)

      e.g.   จำกัด<u>ความ</u>   to give a definition

              ย่อ<u>ความ</u>   to summarize

2. ความ means (legal) case or lawsuit.

      e.g.   สู้<u>ความ</u>   to fight a lawsuit

              ชนะ<u>ความ</u>   to win a lawsuit

3. ความ is a prefix in Thai meaning -ness, -ity, etc.

      3.1   The most frequent use of ความ is as a prefix placed in front of verbs or adjectives to form abstract nouns expressing a state or quality. It is usually rendered in English by such suffixes as -ness, -ity, -ment, -ance, -(t)ion, -ure, -y, -ery, -ship, -dom, -ing and the like.

      e.g.   <u>ความ</u>ดี   goodness, virtue

              <u>ความ</u>ฉลาด   cleverness, intelligence

              <u>ความ</u>สูง   height

              <u>ความ</u>คิด   thought

      3.2   As a bound element, ความ can also be placed before the negative.

      e.g.   <u>ความ</u>ไม่จริง   untruthfulness

              <u>ความ</u>ไม่สะอาด   uncleanliness

<u>ประโยค</u>

1.   ผมไม่มีความรู้สึก

2.   เรามีความหวัง

3.   คนญี่ปุ่นรักความสะอาด

4.   ดิฉันรู้สึกตื่นเต้นมาก

5.   ที่เมืองไทยการแพทย์ยังไม่ดี

6.   อเมริกาใช้เงินกับการทหารมาก

7.   ตอนนี้เมืองไทยเศรษฐกิจไม่ดี

8.   เราควรให้ความสำคัญกับการศึกษา

9.   เขาไม่มีความสำคัญ

10. ผมพยายามจะทำให้สำเร็จ

11. ความพยายามอยู่ที่ไหน ความสำเร็จอยู่ที่นั่น

12. โต๊ะตัวนี้กว้างสองเมตร

13. ถนนเส้นนี้ยาวสิบไมล์

14. มีอะไรกินบ้าง
     คุณจะซื้ออะไรบ้าง

15. คุณควรเรียนภาษาไทย
     คุณต้องเรียนภาษาไทย

16. คุณอยากดื่มอะไร   – อะไรก็ได้

17. คุณอยากไปเที่ยวที่ไหน – ที่ไหนก็ได้

18. ใครก็ได้
     ยังไงก็ได้
     เมื่อไหร่ก็ได้

19. คุณจะไปกับใครก็ได้
     คุณจะไปยังไงก็ได้
     คุณจะไปเมื่อไหร่ก็ได้

20. คุณมีเงินไหม   – มีบ้าง
     คุณชอบอาหารฝรั่งไหม – ชอบบ้าง

บทสนทนา ๑

จูลี่กับสมใจ

จูลี่: ดิฉันอยากซื้อที่ดินสำหรับทำธุรกิจที่เมืองไทย
สมใจ: คุณไม่ใช่คนไทย ซื้อไม่ได้ค่ะ
จูลี่: ทำไมซื้อไม่ได้คะ
สมใจ: กฎหมายไทยไม่ให้ชาวต่างประเทศซื้อ
จูลี่: ไม่ยุติธรรมเลยนะคะ

บทสนทนา ๒

ทานากะกับยุพา

ทานากะ: การศึกษาที่เมืองไทยเป็นยังไงบ้าง
ยุพา: ยังไม่ค่อยดี มีเด็กที่ไม่ได้ไปโรงเรียนอีกมาก
ทานากะ: ผมคิดว่าตอนนี้เศรษฐกิจเมืองไทยดีขึ้นแล้ว
ยุพา: ใช่ แต่รัฐบาลไม่ค่อยให้ความสนใจด้านการศึกษา
 ยังมีคนจนที่ไม่ได้เรียนอีกมาก
 ที่ญี่ปุ่นเป็นยังไงบ้าง
ทานากะ: ผมคิดว่าดี แต่คิดว่าเด็กญี่ปุ่นเรียนหนักเกินไป

บทสนทนา ๓

พิชัยกับจิม

พิชัย:	ตอนนี้ที่บ้านกำลังมีปัญหาครับ
จิม:	ปัญหาอะไรครับ
พิชัย:	คุณพ่อไม่สบายมาก
	ไม่ได้ทำงานสองเดือนแล้ว
จิม:	คุณควรให้คุณพ่อไปหาหมอนะครับ
พิชัย:	อยากพาไป แต่ระยะนี้ไม่มีเงินเลย
จิม:	ผมให้ยืมก่อนได้ครับ
พิชัย:	จริงหรือครับ ขอบคุณมาก

Test 4

Match the English words with the Thai words.

_____	1. width	a.	ตื่นเต้น
_____	2. to try	b.	ผู้จัดการ
_____	3. to hope	c.	ความสำคัญ
_____	4. to feel	d.	เศรษฐกิจ
_____	5. length	e.	ความยากจน
_____	6. education	f.	หวัง
_____	7. to cure	g.	ตรวจ
_____	8. economy	h.	ความยาว
_____	9. manager	i.	นิ้ว
_____	10. to examine	j.	ความรัก
_____	11. success	k.	การศึกษา
_____	12. importance	l.	รู้สึก
_____	13. poverty	m.	ความสูง
_____	14. inch	n.	พยายาม
_____	15. to be excited	o.	เมตร
		p.	ความสำเร็จ
		q.	รักษา
		r.	ความกว้าง

Translate the following into English.

1. เขาไม่มีการศึกษา

   _____

2. คุณควรเรียนภาษาญี่ปุ่น

   _____

3. เราต้องมีความพยายาม

   _____

4. ผมเป็นผู้จัดการร้านอาหารไทย

   _____

5. คุณจะไปที่ไหนบ้าง

   _____

Lesson 5
บทที่ ๕

บทที่ ๕

คำศัพท์
Vocabulary

ที่

ที่   tîi
at, place, space

a. ที่ has many usages depending on its position. Earlier we have used it as a preposition meaning "at", "in" or "to".

e.g.   เขาอยู่ที่บ้าน   He is at home.

เขาอยู่ที่เมืองไทย   He is in Thailand.

b. ที่ is also an initial element meaning "thing where, place where", in certain noun derivatives.

e.g.   ที่เขี่ยบุหรี่   ashtray (a place where cigarette ash goes)

ที่นั่ง   seat (a place to sit)

c. ที่ is used as a classifier of numbers of dishes, cups, seats.

e.g.   ข้าวสองที่   two dishes of rice

ที่นั่งสามที่   three seats

d. ที่ is used as a short form of ที่ดิน (land)

e.g.   เขาซื้อที่   He bought land.

เขาซื้อที่ที่เมืองไทย   He bought land in Thailand.

e. ที่ is used as a pronoun meaning 'that, who, which'

e.g.   คนที่มา   the person who came

คนที่มาชื่อคุณสมชัย   The person who came was Mr. Somchai.

หนังสือที่ผมชอบ   the book that I like

หนังสือที่ผมชอบอยู่บนโต๊ะ The book that I like is on the table.

ที่เกิด tîi-gə̀ət	birthplace, origin
ที่เก็บของ tîi-gèpkɔ̌ɔng	storage place
ที่จอดรถ tîi-jɔ̀ɔt-rót	parking space
ที่ตั้ง tîi-dtâng	location
ที่ทำงาน tîi-tam-ngaan	office, place to work
ที่เที่ยว tîi-tîao	place to tour/go
ที่นอน tîi-nɔɔn	mattress, place to sleep
ที่นา tîi-naa	farm, farmland
ที่ประชุม tîi-bprà-chum	assembly, meeting place
ที่พัก tîi-pák	lodging, resting place
ที่ว่าง tîi-wâang	unoccupied space/place
ที่อยู่ tîi-yùu	address, place to live

ว่า

ว่า wâa   to say, to scold

ว่า may be used either as a verb or as a conjunction. As a verb it means "to say", but its use in this sense is confined to sentences reporting speech.

ว่า usually follows verbs of saying, asking, knowing and it is translated as 'that', 'whether' or not translated at all.

e.g.   พูดว่า   to say (that)
         เขาพูดว่าเขาชอบเมืองไทย He says (that) he likes
                                      Thailand.
         คิดว่า   to think (that)
         เขาคิดว่าเขาชอบเมืองไทย He thinks (that) he likes
                                      Thailand.

พูดว่า/บอกว่า pûut wâa/bɔ̀ɔk wâa to say that

รู้ว่า rúu wâa   to know that

ได้ยินว่า dâi-yin wâa   to hear that

ฝันว่า fǎn wâa   to dream that

เข้าใจว่า kâo-jai wâa   to understand that
สัญญาว่า sǎn-ɏaa wâa   to promise that
ถามว่า tǎam wâa   to ask that/whether
ดูว่า duu wâa   to see that
แปลว่า bplɛɛ wâa   to be translated ...
อ่านว่า àan wâa   to be read ...
เรียกว่า rîak wâa   to be called ...

ถึงแม้ว่า/ถึง tǔng-mɛ́ɛ wâa/tǔng although

เพื่อว่า pɨ̂a wâa   in order that

ถูก

a. ถูก tùuk   cheap

     e.g.   ราคาถูก   low price, cheap

           หนังสือเล่มนี้ถูก   This book is cheap.

b. ถูก tùuk   correct, right

     e.g.   คุณพูดไม่ถูก   You don't say it right.

           ถูกแล้ว   That's right!

c. ถูก tùuk   to touch, to hit (as a target)

     e.g.   ถูกตัว   to touch the body

           ถูกลอตเตอรี่   to win the lottery

d. ถูก tùuk   to come in contact with

     e.g.   ถูกใจ   to please, to one's taste

           คุณถูกใจผมมาก   You are really my taste.

           ถูกคอ   to get along well (because of compatible tastes or interests)

           เราถูกคอกัน   We get along well.

           ถูกชะตา   to appeal to one on first sight

           เราถูกชะตากัน   We get along well.

e. ถูก + verb is also an element used in making the passive voice.

     e.g.   ถูกกิน   to be eaten

           ถูกกัด   to be bitten

           ถูกตี   to be hit

           เขาถูกรถชน   He was hit by a car.

Note: ถูก can be replaced with โดน . e.g. ถูกตี = โดนตี

ถูก unlike passive voice in English is usually used in a negative sense. When the meaning is positive, ได้รับ is used instead of ถูก.

e.g. เขาได้รับรางวัล He was given a prize.

เขาได้รับชม He was praised.

อย่า	yàa	don't
ห้าม	hâam	do not (strong or formal)
อย่าเพิ่ง	yàa pôˆng	Wait!, Don't do that yet!
หยุด	yùt	to stop
เข้า	kâo	to enter
ตี/ชน	dtii/chon	to hit
กัด	gàt	to bite
ราคา	raa-kaa	price
รางวัล	raang-wan	prize
นามบัตร	naambàt	name card
ชม	chom	to praise

ประโยค

1. ไม่มีที่จอดรถ

2. ผมจะไปที่ทำงาน

3. อเมริกามีที่เที่ยวมาก

4. ที่นอนอันนี้เปียก

5. บ้านหลังนี้มีที่ว่าง

6. ผมจะให้ที่อยู่คุณ

7. ดิฉันรู้ว่าเขาจะมา

8. ผมฝันว่าได้ไปเมืองไทย

9. เขาสัญญาว่าจะมาหา

10. "Telephone" แปลว่าอะไร

11. นี่อ่านว่าอะไร

12. ภาษาไทยเรียกว่าอะไร

13. ร้านอาหารนี้ราคาถูก

14. เขาพูดภาษาอังกฤษไม่ค่อยถูก

15. ตีไม่ถูก

16. เขาไม่ค่อยถูกชะตากับผม

17. น้องถูกแม่ตี

18. เขาถูกงูกัด

19. อย่านอนดึก

20. ห้ามเข้า

บทสนทนา ๑

วิไลกับลินดา

วิไล: ขอที่อยู่คุณลินดาที่อเมริกาด้วยค่ะ
ลินดา: ได้ค่ะ นี่นามบัตรของดิฉัน มีที่อยู่กับ
           เบอร์โทรศัพท์
วิไล: ที่เมืองไทยคุณพักที่ไหนคะ
ลินดา: พักกับเพื่อนที่กรุงเทพค่ะ

บทสนทนา ๒

ลอร่ากับโสภา

ลอร่า: นี่อ่านว่าอะไรคะ
โสภา: อ่านว่า "กุม-พา-พัน"
ลอร่า: แปลว่าอะไรคะ
โสภา: แปลว่า "February"
           นี่ภาษาอังกฤษเรียกว่าอะไรคะ
ลอร่า: นี่เรียกว่า "television"
           แปลว่า "โทรทัศน์"

บทสนทนา ๓

สุรีกับดอน

สุรี:   คุณซื้อกระเป๋าใบนั้นที่ไหนครับ

ดอน: ซื้อที่ฮ่องกงครับ

สุรี:   ขอโทษนะครับ ราคาเท่าไหร่ครับ

ดอน: ประมาณสามร้อยบาท

สุรี:   ถูกมาก

ดอน: ใช่ครับ กระเป๋าใบนี้ถูกใจผมมาก
         ราคาไม่แพง แต่ใช้ดี

Test 5

Match the English words with the Thai words.

_____	1. to hit	a.	ที่นา
_____	2. birthplace	b.	ตี
_____	3. to promise that	c.	ฝันว่า
_____	4. meeting place	d.	ที่อยู่
_____	5. to dream that	e.	รางวัล
_____	6. resting place	f.	ที่ทำงาน
_____	7. address	g.	ราคา
_____	8. to bite	h.	ที่ประชุม
_____	9. prize	i.	ถูกลอตเตอรี่
_____	10. parking place	j.	ที่พัก
_____	11. price	k.	การศึกษา
_____	12. office	l.	ที่เกิด
_____	13. unoccupied space	m.	สัญญาว่า
_____	14. to win a lottery	n.	ที่จอดรถ
_____	15. farmland	o.	กัด
		p.	ที่ว่าง
		q.	คิดว่า
		r.	ที่นอน

Translate the following into English.

1.   เขาถามว่าคุณชื่ออะไร

_____

2.   บ้านผมไม่มีที่เก็บของ

_____

3.   เราถูกครูดี

_____

4.   อย่าไปที่นั่นคนเดียว

_____

5.   นี่ภาษาอังกฤษเรียกว่าอะไร

_____

Lesson 6
บทที่ ๖

บทที่ ๖

คำศัพท์   <u>Vocabulary</u>

<u>ใจ</u>

ใจ jai   heart, mind, spirit

* Note: ใจ is "the heart" or "the mind" which is considered the seat of all emotional feeling. It is used as a prefix or suffix with a great number of words (verbs or adjectives) to denote a mental or emotional state.

ใจกว้าง jai-gwâang	generous
ใจแคบ jai-kêɛp	narrow-minded
ใจร้อน jai-rɔ́ɔn	impatient
ใจเย็น jai-yen	calm, cool-headed
ใจแข็ง jai-kɛ̌ng	hard-hearted, unyielding
ใจอ่อน jai-ɔ̀ɔn	soft-hearted, yielding
ใจดำ jai-dam	merciless, mean
ใจดี jai-dii	kind, good-natured
ใจร้าย jai-ráai	unkind, cruel
ใจลอย jai-lɔɔi	absent-minded
ดีใจ dii-jai	glad
เบาใจ bao-jai	relieved
หนักใจ nàkjai	worried
ชื่นใจ chûɯn-jai	pleasant, refreshing
สบายใจ sà-baai-jai	care-free, contented
ภูมิใจ puumjai	proud

นอกใจ	nɔ̂ɔkjai	unfaithful to
พอใจ	pɔɔ-jai	satisfied
ตกใจ	dtòkjai	frightened, scared
มั่นใจ	mân-jai	to have confidence
แน่ใจ	nɛ̂ɛ-jai	to be sure, to be certain
เสียใจ	sǐa-jai	sorry, to feel badly
เอาใจ	ao-jai	to please, indulgent
ตัดสินใจ	dtàtsǐnjai	to decide
ตั้งใจ	dtâng-jai	to intend, to concentrate
สนใจ	sǒnjai	interested
เกรงใจ	greeng-jai	to have consideration for
ตามใจ	dtaamjai	to yield to the wishes of
เจ็บใจ	jèpjai	to have one's feeling hurt
กลุ้มใจ	glûumjai	depressed
เปลี่ยนใจ	bplìanjai	to change one's mind
แปลกใจ	bplɛ̀kjai	surprised
ไว้ใจ	wái-jai	to trust
หายใจ	hǎai-jai	to breath

ขี้

ขี้ kîi	excrement, dung, residue, dirt*
ขี้ kîi	to defecate
ขี้หมู kîi-mǔu	pig dung
ขี้หมา kîi-mǎa	dog dung
ขี้ตา kîi-dtaa	eye mucus
ขี้หู kîi-hǔu	earwax
ขี้เถ้า kîi-tâo	ashes

* Note: ขี้ is also a prefix meaning "characterized by, given to, having a tendency to". It is placed before verbs or adjectives.

ขี้อาย kîi-aai	bashful, shy
ขี้ลืม kîi-lʉʉm	forgetful
ขี้โกง kîi-goong	cheating
ขี้ขอ kîi-kɔ̌ɔ	habitually asking for things
ขี้เหนียว kîi-nǐao	stingy, cheap
ขี้บ่น kîi-bòn	to be given to complaining
ขี้เมา kîi-mao	drunkard
ขี้ยา kîi-yaa	cigarette/drug addict
ขี้เหล้า kîi-lâo	alchohol addict
ขี้หนาว kîi-nǎao	to be sensitive to cold weather
ขี้ร้อน kîi-rɔ́ɔn	to be sensitive to hot weather
ขี้สงสาร kîi-sǒng-sǎan	overly sympathetic

ขี้โรค kîi-rôok	sickly, unhealthy
ขี้สงสัย kîi-sŏng-sǎi	skeptical
ขี้อิจฉา kîi-ìtchǎa	jealous
ขี้ขลาด kîi-klàat	cowardly, timid
ขี้เล่น kîi-lên	playful
ขี้อ้อน kîi-ɔ̂ɔn	to be given to crying, wanting attention
ขี้หึง kîi-hǔng	jealous (of lovers)
ขี้อวด kîi-ùat	boastful
ขี้โกหก kîi-goo-hòk	to be given to telling lies

น่า

น่า nâa   —

* Note: น่า is a prefix added to verbs having the meaning of "should, might like to", or "having the attribute of being_____ able".

น่ากิน nâa-gin	tasty-looking
น่าดื่ม nâa-dùɯm	to look good to drink
น่ารัก nâa-rák	lovely, cute
น่าอยู่ nâa-yùu	cozy, liveable
น่าซื้อ nâa-sɯ́ɯ	worth buying
น่าดู nâa-duu	worth seeing
น่าอ่าน nâa-àan	worth reading
น่ารู้ nâa-rúu	worth learning
น่าลอง nâa-lɔɔng	worth trying
น่าคิด nâa-kít	worth thinking about
น่าฟัง nâa-fang	pleasant to listen to
น่าเชื่อ nâa-chɯ̂a	believable
น่ากลัว nâa-glua	frightening
น่ารำคาญ nâa-ramkaan	annoying
น่าสนใจ nâa-sǒnjai	interesting
น่าเบื่อ naa-bɯ̀a	boring
น่าสงสาร nâa-sǒng-sǎan	pitiful
น่าเสียใจ nâa-sǐa-jai	regrettable
น่าเสียดาย nâa-sǐa-daai	What a pity!
น่าสงสัย nâa-sǒng-sǎi	suspicious

น่านับถือ	nâa-náptǔǔ	worthy of respect
น่าไว้ใจ	nâa-wái-jai	trustworthy
น่าใจหาย	nâa-jai-hǎai	shocking, frightful
น่าเอ็นดู	nâa-enduu	cute (as a child, pet)
น่าชม	nâa-chom	admirable
น่าทึ่ง	nâa-tûng	impressive (colloquial)
ไม่น่าเลย	mâi-nâa-ləəi	It shouldn't have been like that at all!
ไม่น่า/ไม่น่าล่ะ	maî-nâa/mâi-nâa-lâ	No wonder!
แบบไหน	bὲεpnǎi	What type?
คุณล่ะ	kun lâ	and you, what about you
นิสัย	ní-sǎi	behavior, habit
นิสัยดี	ní-sǎi-dii	well-behaved
สุภาพ	sù-pâap	polite
เรียบร้อย	rîaprɔ́ɔi	neat, looking nice
ร่าเริง	râa-rəəng	lively
เห็นแก่ตัว	hěngὲε-dtua	selfish
ไม่เอาไหน	mâi-ao-nǎi	sloppy
เจ้าเล่ห์	jâo-lêe	cunning
ซื่อ/ซื่อตรง	sûu/sûu-dtrong	honest
เกี่ยวกับ	gìao-gàp	about
สำหรับ	sǎmràp	for
เฉยๆ	chɔ̌əi-chɔ̌əi	so-so, just

<u>ประโยค</u>

ใจ

1.   เขาใจกว้าง/เขาเป็นคนใจกว้าง

2.   เขาไม่ใจแคบ/เขาไม่ใช่คนใจแคบ

3.   ผมชอบคนใจเย็น

4.   ใจเย็นๆ อย่าใจร้อน

5.   คุณใจดำมาก

6.   วันนี้สบายใจดี

7.   ผมภูมิใจในตัวคุณมาก

8.   เขานอกใจแฟน

9.   เขาไม่ค่อยพอใจ

10. เสียใจด้วย

11. เขาตั้งใจทำงานดี

12. ผมไม่สนใจ

13. คนนี้เอาใจเก่ง

14. ผมตัดสินใจไม่ได้

15. ผมเกรงใจคุณ

16. ตามใจคุณ

17. เขาทำให้ผมเจ็บใจ

18. ดิฉันกลุ้มใจจริงๆ

19. คุณสมชัยเปลี่ยนใจแล้ว

20. ผมหายใจไม่ออก

ขี้

1. เขาขี้อาย/เขาเป็นคนขี้อาย

2. เขาขี้ลืม/เขาเป็นคนขี้ลืม

3. เขาไม่ขี้โกง/เขาไม่ใช่คนขี้โกง

4. ผมไม่ชอบคนขี้เหนียว

5. คุณขี้บ่นมาก

6. เขาเป็นคนขี้เมา

7. คนนั้นขี้ยา

8. ดิฉันมีแฟนเป็นคนขี้เหล้า

9. ผมเป็นคนขี้หนาว

10. เขาขี้ร้อน

11. ผมไม่ใช่คนขี้โรค

12. เขาไม่เชื่อคุณ เขาขี้สงสัย

13. ดิฉันเป็นคนขี้สงสาร

14. คนนี้ขี้อิจฉา

15. เราไม่ชอบคนขี้ขลาด

16. ผมเป็นคนขี้เล่น

17. แฟนผมขี้อ้อนมาก

18. เขามีสามีขี้หึง

19. คนนั้นขี้อวดจริงๆ

20. ผมไม่ชอบเขา เพราะเขาชอบโกหก

น่า

1. ขนมอันนี้น่ากินมาก

2. เบียร์แก้วนี้น่าดื่ม

3. เขาน่ารัก/เขาเป็นคนน่ารัก

4. เมืองนี้ไม่น่าอยู่

5. กระเป๋าใบนี้น่าซื้อมาก

6. หนังเรื่องนี้ไม่น่าดูเลย

7. หนังสือเล่มนี้น่าอ่านจริงๆ

8. ภาษาไทยน่าลอง

9. ผมมีเรื่องน่าคิด

10. เขาพูดไม่น่าฟัง

11. ไม่น่าเชื่อ

12. น่ากลัวจริงๆ

13. เขาเป็นคนน่ารำคาญ

14. หนังสือเล่มนี้น่าเบื่อ ไม่น่าสนใจเลย

15. เด็กคนนี้น่าสงสารมาก

16. น่าเสียดายที่คุณมาไม่ได้

17. มีอะไรน่าสงสัย

18. เขาเป็นคนน่านับถือ

19. เขาไม่น่าไว้ใจ

20. เด็กคนนี้น่าเอ็นดูจริงๆ

บทสนทนา ๑

จิมกับยุพา

จิม: คุณชอบคนยังไงครับ
ยุพา: ชอบคนสุภาพและใจดี
          และคุณล่ะคะ คุณชอบคนแบบไหน
จิม: ผมชอบคนร่าเริงและใจกว้าง
ยุพา: ฉันคิดว่าคุณจิมเป็นคนน่ารัก
          และสุภาพมากค่ะ
จิม: ขอบคุณครับ ผมก็คิดว่าคุณยุพา
          เรียบร้อย นิสัยดี

บทสนทนา ๒

นิดกับเจมส์

เจมส์:   คุณคิดว่าเขาเป็นคนยังไง
นิด: คิดว่าเขาขี้เหนียวนิดหน่อย
          คุณคิดว่ายังไงคะ
เจมส์:   ไม่รู้ คุณชอบเขาไหม
นิด: เฉยๆ ยังไม่รู้จักเขาดี

<u>บทสนทนา ๓</u>

แซมกับไก่ – ที่ร้านหนังสือ

แซม: หนังสือเล่มนี้น่าอ่านมาก

ไก่:   เกี่ยวกับอะไรครับ

แซม: เกี่ยวกับปัญหาเศรษฐกิจโลก

ไก่:   น่าสนใจนะ คุณจะซื้อไหม

แซม: คิดว่าจะซื้อครับ

ไก่:   ราคาเท่าไหร่

แซม: สองร้อยห้าสิบบาท

ไก่:   คิดว่าแพงเกินไป

แซม: คุณจะซื้อหรือเปล่าครับ

ไก่:   ผมยังไม่อยากซื้อตอนนี้ ขออ่านกับคุณได้ไหม

แซม: ได้ครับ ไม่ต้องเกรงใจ

ไก่:   ขอบคุณมากครับ

Test 6

Match the English words with the Thai words.

_____	1. sensitive to hot weather	a.	ใจร้าย
_____	2. mean	b.	ขี้ร้อน
_____	3. to have a consideration for	c.	เกรงใจ
_____	4. What a pity!	d.	น่าเบื่อ
_____	5. bashful	e.	ใจดำ
_____	6. to decide	f.	น่าดู
_____	7. liveable	g.	ขี้เหนียว
_____	8. jealous	h.	น่ารำคาญ
_____	9. absent-minded	i.	ขี้เมา
_____	10. annoying	j.	ตัดสินใจ
_____	11. lovely	k.	ขี้หึง
_____	12. worth watching	l.	น่ารัก
_____	13. worried	m.	หนักใจ
_____	14. cruel	n.	ขี้ขอ
_____	15. drunkard	o.	ใจลอย
		p.	น่าอยู่
		q.	น่าเสียดาย
		r.	ขี้อาย

Translate the following into English.

1. วันนี้น่าเบื่อมาก

    _____

2. เขาขี้ลืม

    _____

3. อย่าใจลอย

    _____

4. ดิฉันชอบคนใจเย็น

    _____

5. ผมมีแฟนขี้บ่น

    _____

Lesson 7
บทที่ ๗

บทที่ ๗

คำศัพท์	Vocabulary
ชื่อ chûu	name
ชื่อจริง chûu-jing	official name
ชื่อเล่น chûu-lên	nickname
นามสกุล naamsà-gun	family name
เซ็นชื่อ senchûu	to sign name
รายชื่อ raai-chûu	list of names
นาย naai	Mr.
นาง nang	Mrs.
นางสาว nang-sǎao	Miss
ของจริง kɔ̌ɔng-jing	real thing
ของปลอม kɔ̌ɔng-bplɔɔm	false/fake thing
ของเล่น kɔ̌ɔng-lên	toy
รายการอาหาร/เมนู	menu
raai-gaan aa-hǎan/mee-nuu	
สั่ง sàng	order
เช็ค/ตรวจ chék/dtrùat	check
เช็คบิล chékbin	to check the bill
ไม้จิ้มฟัน mái-jîmfan	toothpick
ร้องไห้ rɔ́ɔng-hâi	to cry
หัวเราะ hǔa-rɔ́	to laugh
ลืม luum	to forget

ทำหาย tamhǎai	to lose
ทำ....หาย tam...hǎai	to lose (something)
ค้น kón	to search
หา hǎa	to look for
หาเจอ hǎa-jəə	to find
หาไม่เจอ hǎa-mâi-jəə	cannot find
เห็นด้วย (กับ) hěndûai (gàp)	to agree (with)
หิว/หิวข้าว hǐu/hǐu-kâao	hungry
หิวน้ำ hǐu-náam	thirsty
อิ่ม ìm	full (stomach)
เยอะ/เยอะๆ/เยอะแยะ yə́/yə́-yə́/yə́-yɛ́	a lot
ต่อไป dtɔɔ-bpai	next
ระวัง rá-wang	careful, to watch out
ตามสบาย dtaam sa-baai	Do as you please!

Some Common Thai Dishes

ต้มยำกุ้ง	dtôm-yamgûng	lemon grass shrimp soup
ต้มข่าไก่	dtômkàa-gài	galanga chicken soup
แกงจืด	gɛɛng-jùut	mild soup with vegetables & pork
ยำเนื้อ	yamnúa	spicy beef salad
ยำวุ้นเส้น	yamwúnsên	bean thread salad
ยำมะเขือ	yammá-kǔa	spicy eggplant salad
ลาบเนื้อ	lâapnúa	spicy beef salad
ส้มตำ	sôm-dtam	spicy green papaya salad
ปอเปี๊ยะ	bpɔɔ-bpía	spring rolls
สะเต๊ะ	sà-dté	satay
แกงเผ็ด	gɛɛng-pèt	curry, red curry
แกงเขียวหวาน	gɛɛng-kǐao-wǎan	green curry
แกงป่า	gɛɛng-bpàa	country style curry
แกงส้ม	gɛɛng-sôm	sour fish curry
ไก่ย่าง	gài-yâang	chicken barbecue
ไก่ผัดขิง	gài-pàtkǐng	fried chicken with ginger
กุ้งผัดพริกเผา	gûng-pàtpríkpǎo	fried prawn with chillies
ปลาหมึกผัดเผ็ด	bplaa-mùk pàt-pèt	spicy fried squid
ขนมจีน	kà-nǒmjiin	Thai vermicilli
ผัดเปรี้ยวหวาน	pàt-bprîao-waan	fried sweet and sour
ผัดไทย	pàt-tai	Thai fried noodles
ข้าวผัด	kâao-pàt	fried rice
ข้าวผัดกุ้ง	kâao-pàtgûng	fried rice with shrimp

ข้าวสวย kâao-sǔai   steamed rice
ข้าวเหนียว kâao-nǐao   sticky rice
ข้าวต้ม kâao-dtôm   rice porridge
ข้าวต้มหมู kâao-dtômmǔu   rice porridge with pork
ไข่เจียว kài-jiao   omelette
ไข่ดาว kài-daao   sunny side-up
ไข่ต้ม kài-dtôm   boiled egg

ของหวาน **Desserts**

ข้าวเหนียวมะม่วง   sticky rice with mango
   kâao-nǐao-má-mûang
สะหริ่ม sà-rìm   jelly pea flour with coconut
                                       milk
ตะโก้ dtà-gôo   Thai jelly with coconut
                                       cream
ข้าวหลาม kâao-lǎam   sticky rice and coconut in
                                       bamboo
ข้าวเหนียวดำ kâao-nǐao-dam   black rice pudding
กล้วยบวชชี glûai-bùatchii   banana in coconut milk
กล้วยเชื่อม gûai-chûeam   banana stewed in syrup
สังขยา sǎng-kà-yǎa   coconut custard
หม้อแกง mɔ̂ɔ-gɛɛng   egg custard
ฝอยทอง fɔ̌ɔi-tɔɔng   sweet shredded egg yolk
ไอติม/ไอสครีม ai-dtim/ai-sà-kriim   ice cream

Names

Most Thai people have nicknames in addition to their official names. The nicknames do not necessarily come from their official names. When you know them well, Thai people prefer to be called by their nicknames. If they are close enough to you or younger than you, they may call themselves by their nicknames instead of using other pronouns.

Some Thai nicknames have meanings, and some don't. Treat them as mere names—don't try to translate the names because some might be funny or not make any sense.

Some Common Thai Nicknames

เล็ก	lék	น้อย	nɔ́ɔi	หน่อย	nɔ̀i
ใหญ่	yài	แดง	dɛɛng	ดำ	dam
ตุ๊กตา	dtùk-dtaa	แหม่ม	mɛ̀m	หมู	mǔu
ไก่	gài	หนึ่ง	nùng	เป็ด	bpèt
แมว	mɛɛo	เหมียว	mǐao	แก้ว	gɛ̂ɛo
กุ้ง	gûng	นก	nók	หนู	nǔu
มด	mót	กบ	gòp	เอ๋	ěe
อั้น	ǎn	โอ๋	ǒo	เปี๊ยก	bpíak
แจง	jɛɛng	เจี๊ยบ	jíap	นุช	nút
ต๋ิม	dtǐm	ต้อย	dtɔ̂i	นิด	nít
ใหม่	mài	จิ๋ม	jǐm	หนิง	nǐng
บุ๋ม	bǔm	ตั๊ก	dtík	จุ๋ม	jǔm
เปิ้ล	bpə̂n	โต้ง	dtôong	ตุ๊ย	dtúi
ตุ๋ย	dtǔi	ส้ม	sôm	โจ้	jôo
ฝน	fǒn	ฟ้า	fáa	อ้อ	ɔ̂ɔ
แอน	ɛɛn	เดือน	dtɯan	ต้น	dtón
ต๋ิง	dtǐng	อุ๋ย	ǔi	อุ๊ด	úut

Some Common Thai First Names

Thai has many first names. Here are some common ones that you can practice reading.

กมล	gà-mon	กรรณิการ์	ganní-gaa
กาญจนา	gaanjà-naa	เกษม	gà-sěem
เกรียงศักดิ์	griang-sàk	ขวัญชัย	kwǎn-chai
จรัญ	jà-ran	จารุวรรณ	jaa-rú-wan
จินตนา	jin-dtà-naa	ฉวีวรรณ	chà-wǐi-wan
ชัยชาญ	chai-chaan	ชำนาญ	chamnaan
ดวงใจ	duang-jai	ดารณี	daa-rá-nii
ดำรงค์	damrong	ถนอม	tà-nɔ̌ɔm
ถาวร	tǎa-wɔɔn	ทนงศักดิ์	tá-nong-sàk
ทัศนีย์	tátsà-nii	ธงชัย	tong-chai
ธวัช	tá-wát	ธานี	taa-nii
ธิดา	tí-daa	นคร	ná-kɔɔn
ณรงค์	ná-rong	นงลักษญ์	nong-lák
นพดล	nóppá-don	นฤมล	ná-rɨ́-mon
นวลจันทร์	nuanjan	นิคม	ní-kom
นิตยา	nít-dtà-yaa	บัญชา	banchaa
บุญชู	bunchuu	เบญจวรรณ	benjà-wan
ประกิต	bprà-gìt	ประจักษ์	bprà-jàk
ประชา	bprà-chaa	ประทุม	bprà-tum
ประไพ	bprà-pai	ประภา	bprà-paa
ปัญญา	bpan-yaa	ปราณี	bpraa-nii
ปรีชา	bprii-chaa	พงศักดิ์	pongsàk

พรชัย	pɔɔnchai	พรทิพย์	pɔɔntíp
พรรณี	pannii	พิชัย	pí-chai
เพ็ญศรี	pensǐi	ไพบูลย์	paiboon
ไพโรจน์	pai-rôot	มนตรี	mon-dtrii
มนัส	má-nát	มยุรี	má-yú-rii
มานี	maa-nii	มานะ	maa-ná
มานิตย์	maa-nít	มาลี	maa-lii
ยุพา	yú-paa	ยุพิน	yú-pin
รัชนี	rátchá-nii	รัตนา	rát-dtà-naa
ละมัย	lá-mai	ลัดดา	látdaa
วัฒนา	wáttá-naa	วรรณี	wannii
วราภรณ์	wá-raa-pɔɔn	วันเพ็ญ	wanpen
วาสนา	wâatsà-nǎa	วิเชียร	wí-chian
วิชัย	wí-chai	วิทยา	wít-tá-yaa
วินัย	wí-nai	วิโรจน์	wí-rôt
วิไล	wí-lai	วิสุทธิ์	wí-sùt
วีระชัย	wii-rá-chai	ศราวุธ	sà-raa-wút
ศศิธร	sà-sì-tɔɔn	ศิริชัย	sì-rì-chai
ศิริพร	sì-rì-pɔɔn	ศักดา	sàkdaa
สกล	sà-gon	สมใจ	sǒmjai
สมชาย	sǒmchaai	สมชัย	sǒmchai
สมทรง	sǒmsong	สมพร	sǒmpɔɔn
สมพงษ์	sǒmpong	สมหมาย	sǒmmǎai
สมศรี	sǒm-sǐi	สมศักดิ์	sǒmsàk
สวัสดิ์	sà-wàt	สำราญ	sǎmraan
สุกัญญา	sù-gan-yaa	สุชาดา	sù-chaa-daa

สุชาติ	sù-châat	สุดา	sù-daa
สุทัศน์	sù-tát	สุเทพ	sù-têep
สุธรรม	sù-tam	สุนันท์	sù-nan
สุนันทา	sù-nan-taa	สุนีย์	sù-nii
สุพจน์	sù-pót	สุภา	sù-paa
สุภาภรณ์	sù-paa-pɔɔn	สุรชัย	sù-rá-chai
สุวรรณ	sù-wan	สุวรรณา	sù-wannaa
สุวิทย์	sù-wít	โสภา	sŏo-paa
ไสว	sà-wǎi	อดิศักดิ์	à-dì-sàk
อดุลย์	à-dun	อนงค์	à-nong
อนันต์	à-nan		

Some English Names Transliterated Into Thai

Here is how some English names are written in Thai. With foreign names, tones are sometimes pronounced differently from how they are written.

Alan	อลัน	Albert	อัลเบิร์ต
Alex	อเล็กซ์	Ann	แอน
Anna	แอนนา	Barbara	บาร์บาร่า
Barry	แบรี่	Becky	เบ็กกี้
Beth	เบธ	Betty	เบตตี้
Bill	บิล	Bob	บ๊อบ
Bobby	บ๊อบบี้	Brian	ไบรอัน
Bruce	บรูซ	Caren/Karen	แคเรน
Carol/Carrol	แครอล	Charlie	ชาลี
Cherry	เชอรี่	Chris	คริส
Christina	คริสตีน่า	Connie	คอนนี่
Craig	เคร้ก	Dan	แดน
Daniel	แดนเนียล	Dave	เดฟ
David	เดวิด	Debbie	เดบบี่
Denny	เดนนี่	Dick	ดิ๊ก
Don	ดอน	Donna	ดอนน่า
Earl	เอิร์ล	Eric	เอริค
Eva	อีวา	Eve	อีฟ
Frank	แฟรงค์	Fred	เฟรด
Gary	แกรี่	George	จอร์จ
Hal	แฮล	Harry	แฮรี่
Helen	เฮเลน	Isaac	ไอแซค
Jack	แจ๊ค	James	เจมส์
Jane	เจน	Janet	เจเน็ต

Jeffrey	เจฟฟรี่	Jennifer	เจนนิเฟอร์
Jerry	เจอรี่	Jenny	เจนนี่
Jessy	เจสซี่	Jinny	จินนี่
Jim	จิม	Jimmy	จิมมี่
Joe	โจ	Joey	โจอี้
John	จอห์น	Johnny	จอห์นนี่
Jody	โจดี้	Judy	จูดี้
Julie	จูลี่	Kate	เคท
Kathy	แคตี้	Kelly	เคลลี่
Ken	เคน	Kevin	เควิน
Kim	คิม	Larry	แลรี่
Linda	ลินดา	Lindsay	ลินซี่
Lisa	ลิซ่า	Lora	ลอร่า
Lori	ลอรี่	Mark	มาร์ค
Mary	แมรี่	Michael	ไมเคิล
Michelle	มิเชล	Nancy	แนนซี่
Pam	แพม	Pat	แพท
Paul	พอล, ปอล	Paula	พอลล่า
Peter	ปีเตอร์	Philip	ฟีลิป
Randy	แรนดี้	Richard	ริชาร์ด
Rick	ริค	Robert	โรเบิร์ต
Ron	รอน	Ruth	รูธ, รูท
Sam	แซม	Sandra	แซนดร้า
Sandy	แซนดี้	Scott	สกอต
Steve	สตีฟ	Stephanie	สเตฟานี
Sue	ซู	Susan/Suzanne	ซูซาน
Tim	ทิม	Tom	ทอม
Tony	โทนี่	Tricia	ทริเชีย
William	วิลเลียม	Wymond	วายมอนด์

<u>ประโยค</u>

1.   คุณ (มี) ชื่อจริงว่าอะไร/ชื่อจริงอะไร
      -ผมมีชื่อจริงว่ามานะ
      -ชื่อว่าเดวิด

2.   มีชื่อเล่นไหม
      -มี ชื่อว่าเล็ก

3.   คุณนามสกุลอะไร
      -นามสกุลพีระ

4.   กรุณาเซ็นชื่อ

5.   อันนี้ของปลอม ไม่ใช่ของจริง

6.   เด็กๆชอบของเล่น

7.   ขอเมนูด้วย

8.   เช็กบิลด้วย

9.   ขอไม้จิ้มฟันหน่อย

10. น้อยร้องไห้

11. ไก่หัวเราะ

12. เขาลืมคุณแล้ว

13. นกทำเงินหาย

14. ผมหาคุณไม่เจอ

15. เห็นด้วย/เห็นด้วยกับคุณ

16. หิวข้าวจริงๆ

17. หิวน้ำไหม   -หิว

18. อิ่มรึยัง   -อิ่มแล้ว

19. อยากมีเงินเยอะๆ

20. มีคนเยอะแยะ

บทสนทนา ๑

เคนกับนุช

เคน:	สวัสดีครับ คุณชื่ออะไรครับ
นุช:	ชื่อนุชค่ะ
เคน:	นุชเป็นชื่อจริงหรือชื่อเล่นครับ
นุช:	ชื่อเล่นค่ะ ดิฉันชื่อจริงว่าสุชาดา คุณชื่ออะไรคะ
เคน:	ผมชื่อเคนครับ ไม่มีชื่อเล่น คุณนามสกุล อะไรครับ
นุช:	นามสกุลแสนเมืองค่ะ

บทสนทนา ๒

วินัยกับไมเคิล–ที่ร้านอาหาร

วินัย:	วันนี้จะสั่งอะไรครับ
ไมเคิล:	อยากทานต้มยำกุ้งกับส้มตำ คุณล่ะครับ
วินัย:	ผมอยากทานผัดไทยครับ คุณจะทานของหวานไหม
ไมเคิล:	วันนี้ไม่อยากทานของหวาน ตามสบายเลยครับ
วินัย:	ครับ ผมอยากทานข้าวเหนียวมะม่วง

<u>บทสนทนา ๓</u>

ใหม่กับโจ

โจ: ใหม่ ทำไมร้องไห้
ใหม่:   ใหม่ทำกระเป๋าเงินหายค่ะ
โจ: ทำหายที่ไหน
ใหม่:   คิดว่าที่ตลาด ตอนเช้านี้มีคนเยอะจริงๆ
โจ: เสียใจด้วยนะ น่าเสียดายจัง ต่อไปต้องระวังนะ

Test 7

Match the English words with the Thai words.

_____ 1. a lot	a.	หิวข้าว
_____ 2. toy	b.	รายการอาหาร
_____ 3. name list	c.	อิ่ม
_____ 4. hungry	d.	ชื่อจริง
_____ 5. to laugh	e.	เยอะๆ
_____ 6. thirsty	f.	หิวน้ำ
_____ 7. full	g.	เห็นด้วย
_____ 8. to agree	h.	ทำหาย
_____ 9. official name	i.	จำได้
_____ 10. to sign name	j.	ลืม
_____ 11. to forget	k.	ร้องไห้
_____ 12. to lose	l.	หัวเราะ
_____ 13. to look for	m.	ของจริง
_____ 14. menu	n.	เซ็นชื่อ
_____ 15. to cry	o.	ของเล่น
	p.	หา
	q.	รายชื่อ
	r.	ของปลอม

Translate the following into English.

1.   คุณทำหนังสือหายเมื่อไหร่

_____

2.   เขาหัวเราะเสียงดัง

_____

3.   อย่าซื้อของปลอม

_____

4.   เขาไม่เห็นด้วยกับผม

_____

5.   ผมลืมไปซื้อของ

_____

Lesson 8
บทที่ ๘

บทที่ ๘

คำศัพท์	<u>Vocabulary</u>

ญาติ yâat	relative
พ่อแม่ pɔ̂ɔ-mɛ̂ɛ	parents
ลูกพี่ลูกน้อง lûukpîi-lûuknɔ́ɔng	cousin
หลาน lǎan	grandchild, nephew, niece
หลานชาย lǎanchaai	grandson, nephew
หลานสาว lǎansǎao	granddaughter, niece
ลูกบุญธรรม lûukbuntam	adopted child
เป็นโสด/โสด bpensòot/sòot	single
ชายโสด chaai-sòot	single man
หญิงโสด yǐng-sòot	single woman
เป็นม่าย bpenmâai	widowed
พ่อม่าย pɔ̂ɔ-mâai	widower
แม่ม่าย mɛ̂ɛ-mâai	widow
พ่อตา pɔ̂ɔ-dtaa	father-in-law (wife's father)
แม่ยาย mɛ̂ɛ-yaai	mother-in-law (wife's mother)
พ่อปู่ pɔ̂ɔ-bpùu	father-in-law (husband's father)
แม่ย่า mɛ̂ɛ-yâa	mother-in-law (husband's mother)
พี่เขย/น้องเขย pîi-kə̌əi/nɔ́ɔng-kə̌əi	brother-in-law
พี่สะใภ้/น้องสะใภ้ pîi-sà-pái/nɔ́ɔng-sà-pái	sister-in-law

ลูกเขย lûukkɔ̌əi   son-in-law

ลูกสะใภ้ lûuksà-pái   daughter-in-law

งานแต่งงาน ngaan-dtɛ̀ng-ngaan   wedding ceremony

พิธี pí-tii   ceremony

หมั้น mân   to engage

คู่หมั้น kûu-mân   fiance, fiancee

แต่งงานใหม่ dtɛ̀ng-ngaanmài   to remarry

เจ้าบ่าว jâo-bàao   bridegroom

เจ้าสาว jâo-sǎao   bride

เพื่อนเจ้าบ่าว pʉ̂anjâo-bàao   best man

เพื่อนเจ้าสาว pʉ̂anjâo-sǎao   bridesmaid

หย่า yàa   to divorce

พระ prá   monk

พระเจ้า prá-jâao   God

โบสถ์ bòot   church

แบบ/สไตล์ bɛ̀ɛp/sà-dtaai   style

จัด jàt   to arrange

นับถือ náptʉ̌ʉ   to respect, to believe in

ศาสนา sàatsà-nǎa   religion

ศาสนาพุทธ sàatsà-nǎa-pút   Buddhism

ศาสนาคริสต์ sàatsà-nǎa-krít   Christianity

ศาสนาอิสลาม sàatsà-nǎa-ìtsà-laam   Islam

ชาวพุทธ chaao-pút   Buddhist

ส่วนมาก sùanmâak   most

นิสัย ní-sǎi   habit, trait

งานเลี้ยง ngaanlíang   party, wedding reception

คำสรรพนาม **Pronouns**

The correct use of Thai pronouns requires a sense of relative age, social status, and respect. Some pronouns can be used in a variety of ways depending on the context. For example, พี่ can be used for first, second or third person. The following points out how the most common pronouns are used.

I /Me

The following are used as 'I' or 'me'.

1. ผม is used by men only. It is the most convenient word for men. It can be used in any occasion and with almost anybody.

e.g.   ผมชอบสีดำ   I like black.

         เขาชอบผม   He likes me.

2. ดิฉัน/ ดิชั้น is used by women only. It is rather formal. When you get to know the person you are talking to well, you can change to other pronouns.

e.g.   ดิฉันชื่อสมใจ   My name is Somjai.

         คุณมาหาดิฉัน   You came to see me.

3. ฉัน/ ชั้น is the short form of ดิฉัน and is used primarily by women. It is less formal than ดิฉัน . You can use this with your friends or acquaintaces.

e.g.   ฉันเป็นคนไทย   I am Thai.
        คุณรักฉัน   You love me.

4. หนู is mostly used by women or very young children. The
speaker must be younger than the one he/she is talking to in order
to use this word.

e.g.   หนูเป็นนักเรียน   I am a student.
        แม่ตีหนู   My mother hit me.

5. เรา can be used as a singular first person as well as a plural
first person by both men and women. The speaker and the listener are usually friends or about the same age. You don't use this
word when you talk to older people or those of higher status.

e.g.   เราชอบกินขนม   I like to eat snacks.
        เขาทำงานให้เรา   He works for me.

6. Using the first person's name or nickname. When you are
close to who you are talking to and you are either younger or
about the same age, you can call yourself by your name or nickname instead of one of the 'I' pronouns. Also younger members
of a family will use their nicknames when they talk to their parents, older brothers and sisters. Men don't tend to call themselves
by their nicknames as often as women.

e.g.   เล็กไปโรงเรียน   I go to school.
        คุณชอบเล็กไหม   Do you like me?

7. พี่ is used when the speaker is older than the listener. It can also be used in front of the speaker's name. You use this when you know the listener well or you want to have a less formal relationship with him or her.

e.g.   พี่จะทำงาน   I am going to work.

         เขาชอบพี่   He likes me.

8. น้อง is used when the speaker is younger than the listener. It can also be used in front of the speaker's name, but not very often. You use this when you know the listener well or you want to have a less formal relationship with him or her.

e.g.   น้องชื่อไก่   My name is Gai.

         คุณพูดกับน้อง   You talk to me.

9. ข้าพเจ้า is used by both men and women in very formal speech, usually by public speakers or writers. It is very rare. Almost nobody uses this word in normal speech.

e.g.   ข้าพเจ้ารักเมืองไทย   I love Thailand.

         กรุณาเชื่อข้าพเจ้า   Please believe me.

10. กู is an old way of addressing oneself used by men and women. It is considered a very impolite way to address oneself nowadays. However, some close friends still like to use it when they talk to each other. Foreigners should not use this word.

e.g.   กูจะอยู่ที่นี่   I will stay here.

         โทรมาหากู   Give me a call.

We /Us

The following are used as 'we' or 'us'.

1. เรา/ พวกเรา/ พวก is a plural first person used by men or women for any occasion.

e.g.   เราชอบกินขนม   We like to eat snacks.

เขาทำงานให้เรา   He works for us.

พวกพี่อยู่ที่อเมริกา   We live in America.

คุณพูดกับพวกพี่   You speak to us.

2. พวก + ชื่อ (the speaker's name , nickname or other pronoun) is a plural first person used by both men and women.

e.g.   พวกหนูชอบไปที่นั่น We like to go there.

เขารักพวกเล็ก   They love us.

You

The following are used as 'you'.

1. คุณ is used to address the person you talk to by both men and women. It is a convenient pronoun in both formal and informal speech.

e.g. คุณทำงานที่ไหน   Where do you work?

ผมรักคุณ   I love you.

2. เธอ is used to address the person you talk to by both men and women, but is for informal use only. It is usually used with people of the same age or by the older speaker.

e.g. เธอชื่ออะไร   What's your name?

ฉันรักเธอ   I love you.

3. หนู is used to address younger women or young children. The speaker must be older than the one he/she is talking to.

e.g. หนูชื่ออะไร   What's your name?

แม่ไม่รักหนู   Mom doesn't love you.

4. เรา is used to address younger people — men and women, singular or plural. It implies some sense of superiority in the speaker.

e.g.   เราชื่ออะไร   What's your name?

          ฉันไม่ชอบเรา   I don't like you.

5. **Using the second person's name or nickname.** You call people whom you are addressing by their names or nicknames when you are close to or know them well. You have to be either older or about the same age to call people by their names. Also older members of a family will address the younger members by their nicknames.

e.g.   เล็กจะไปไหน   Where are you going?

          ผมชอบเล็กมาก   I like you very much.

6. พี่ is used when addressing an older person. It can also be used in front of the listener's name. You use พี่ when you know the listener well or you want to have a less formal relationship with him or her.

e.g.   พี่จะไปไหน   Where are you going?

          หนูชอบพี่เล็ก   I like you.

7. น้อง is used when addressing a younger speaker. It can also be used in front of the listener's name, but not very often. You use this when you know the listener well or you want to have a less formal relationship with him or her. Many times น้อง can be used to call waiters, waitresses, bell boys in hotels, etc.

e.g.   น้องจะไปไหน   Where are you going?

    พี่ชอบน้อง   I like you.

8. ท่าน is a second person pronoun used when you talk to highly respected people such as monks, court judges, royal family members, etc.

e.g.   ท่านจะไปไหน   Where are you going?

    เขาจะมาหาท่าน   He will come to see you.

9. เอ็ง/มึง are old ways of addressing people. Nowadays, they are considered very impolite. However, some close friends still like to use them when they talk to each other. Foreigners should not use these words.

e.g.   เอ็งจะไปไหน   Where are you going?

    กูจะไปหามึง   I am going to see you.

He/Him

The following are used as 'he' or 'him'.

1. เขา/เค้า is used to refer to the third person in general.

e.g.   เขาจะไปไหน   Where is he going?

         เราคุยกับเขา   We talk to him.

2. มัน is normally used to refer to animals or things. It is considered very insulting when you use this to refer to people.

e.g.   มันไม่ดี   He is bad. (Insulting)

         ฉันเกลียดมัน   I hate him. (Insulting)

She/Her

The following are used as 'she' or 'her'.

1. เขา/เค้า is used to refer to the third person.

e.g.   เขาจะไปไหน   Where is she going?

เราคุยกับเขา   We talk to her.

2. เธอ is a singular third person for woman only. It is not used as often as เขา/เค้า , and is usually seen in written language.

e.g.   เธอจะไปไหน   Where is she going?

เราคุยกับเธอ   We talk to her.

3. มัน is considered very insulting when you use it to refer to people.

e.g.   มันไม่ดี   She is bad. (Insulting)

ฉันเกลียดมัน   I hate her. (Insulting)

It

The following are used as 'it'.

1. มัน is used to refer to an animal or a thing.

e.g.   มันไม่ดี   It's bad.

ฉันเกลียดมัน   I hate it.

They /Them

The following are used as 'they' or 'them'.

1. เขา/ พวกเขา are used to refer to the third person in general.

e.g.   <u>เขา</u>จะไปไหน   Where are they going?

        เราคุยกับ<u>พวกเขา</u>   We talk to them.

2. มัน/ พวกมัน are used to refer to plural third persons —
animals, things or people. When they are used to refer to people
they are considered insulting.

e.g.   <u>มัน</u>ไม่ดี   They are bad. (Insulting)

        ฉันเกลียด<u>พวกมัน</u>   I hate them. (Insulting)

Note: Family relationship terms (e.g. ตา, ยาย, ลุง, ป้า, น้า, อา, หลาน,
etc.) are also used as pronouns when appropriate for first, second
or third person. (Look at Lesson 9 in "Thai for Beginners" for
more basic vocabulary about family.)
        There are many pronouns in the Thai language in addition
to those covered above. It is not necessary to memorize them all
at this time — those given above will suffice for virtually any situation that you may encounter.

<u>ประโยค</u>

1. ผมมีญาติที่อเมริกา

2. ฉันคิดถึงพ่อแม่

3. ไก่เป็นลูกพี่ลูกน้องกับแดง

4. นี่หลานชายผม

5. น้อยยังเป็นโสด

6. คุณเดวิดเป็นม่าย

7. พ่อตาของฉันใจดีมาก

8. ลูกสะใภ้กับแม่ย่าไม่ค่อยชอบกัน

9. เรามีพี่เขยฝรั่ง

10. เขาจะแต่งงานใหม่

11. พรุ่งนี้ผมจะไปงานแต่งงานเพื่อน

12. แอนจะเป็นเพื่อนเจ้าสาว

13. คุณวิไลหย่ากับสามีแล้ว

14. จะทำพิธีแบบไทย

15. พระทำพิธีให้เรา

16. คริสเตียนนับถือพระเจ้า

17. พวกเขาแต่งงานที่โบสถ์

18. คุณนับถือศาสนาอะไร
    – ผมนับถือศาสนาคริสต์

19. เขาไม่มีศาสนา

20. คนไทยส่วนมากนับถือศาสนาพุทธ

บทสนทนา ๑

ประชากับบิล

ประชา: ขอโทษครับ คุณบิลแต่งงานรึยังครับ
บิล: แต่งแล้วครับ ภรรยาผมเป็นคนไทย
ประชา: คุณมีญาติที่เมืองไทยไหมครับ
บิล: ไม่มีครับ มีแต่ภรรยาและลูกสองคน
ประชา: คุณนับถือศาสนาอะไรครับ
บิล: ศาสนาคริสต์ครับ แต่ครอบครัวที่นี่
นับถือศาสนาพุทธ

บทสนทนา ๒

ชาลีกับธานี

ชาลี: วันนี้ผมจะไปงานแต่งงาน
ธานี: งานแต่งงานของใครครับ
ชาลี: คุณน้อยกับแฟนชื่อบุญชู
ธานี: งานจัดที่ไหนครับ
ชาลี: ตอนเช้าจัดที่บ้าน ตอนเย็นจัดงานเลี้ยงที่
โรงแรมดุสิต

<u>บทสนทนา ๓</u>

แดงกับแจ็ค

แจ็ค: แดงชอบพวกคุณสมชายไหม

แดง: ชอบมาก แดงคิดว่าพวกเขานิสัยดี

        แจ็คคิดว่ายังไง

แจ็ค: ผมไม่รู้ ยังไม่รู้จักพวกเขาดี

แดง: แดงชอบคุณสมชายที่สุด ทำงานกับเขา

        หลายปีแล้ว แดงคิดว่าแจ็คก็จะชอบเขาด้วย

Test 8

Match the English words with the Thai words.

_____	1. widow	a.	พิธี
_____	2. niece	b.	หลานชาย
_____	3. relative	c.	แม่ม่าย
_____	4. bridegroom	d.	ลูกสะใภ้
_____	5. son-in-law	e.	ตำบล
_____	6. single	f.	แม่ยาย
_____	7. to divorce	g.	ลูกเขย
_____	8. ceremony	h.	แต่งงานใหม่
_____	9. mother-in-law	i.	พระ
_____	10. to remarry	j.	เจ้าสาว
_____	11. religion	k.	พี่สะใภ้
_____	12. church	l.	หย่า
_____	13. sister-in-law	m.	เจ้าบ่าว
_____	14. bride	n.	ศาสนา
_____	15. monk	o.	ญาติ
		p	โสด
		q.	โบสถ์
		r.	หลานสาว

Translate the following into English.

1.   เขามีหลานชายที่เมืองไทย

_____

2.   คุณจอห์นแต่งงานใหม่   แฟนคนใหม่เป็นคนไทย

_____

3.   เจ้าบ่าวหล่อ   เจ้าสาวก็สวย

_____

4.   ฉันนับถือศาสนาอิสลาม

_____

5.   ผมเป็นญาติกับเขา

_____

Lesson 9
บทที่ ๙

บทที่ ๙

คำศัพท์   Vocabulary

ตัว dtua	body, self
ตัวเอง/เอง dtua-eeng/eeng	one's self
ด้วยตัวเอง/เอง dûai-dtua-eeng/eeng	by oneself
ตัวหนังสือ/ตัว dtua-nǎng-sǔʉ/dtua	letter of the alphabet
ตัวเลข dtua-lêek	numeral figure
ตัวอย่าง dtua-yàang	sample, example
ยกตัวอย่าง yók-dtua-yàang	to give an example
ตัวแทน dtua-tɛɛn	representative, agent
ตัวตลก dtua-dtà-lòk	clown, jester
เคยตัว kəəi-dtua	to get into the habit of
เคยชิน/เคย/ชิน kəəi-chin/kəəi/chin	to get used to
เจ็บตัว jèp-dtua	to get hurt
ขอตัว kɔ̌ɔ-dtua	to excuse oneself
ทำตัว tam-dtua	to behave
ประจำตัว bprà-jam-dtua	individual, private
รู้ตัว rúu-dtua	to be aware
รู้สึกตัว rúu-sʉ̀k-dtua	to come to feel, to recover consciousness
เล่นตัว lên-dtua	to play hard to get
ส่วนตัว sùan-dtua	private, personal
ส่วนรวม sùanruam	public, collective
เสียตัว sǐa-dtua	to lose one's virginity
หมดตัว mòt-dtua	to be broke

ตั๋ว dtǔa	ticket
ตั๋วเที่ยวเดียว dtǔa-tîao-diao	one-way ticket
ตั๋วไป-กลับ dtǔa-bpai-glàp	round-trip ticket
คนขายตั๋ว konkǎai-dtǔa	ticket seller
บัตร bàt	card, ticket
บัตรเชิญ bàtchəən	invitation card
บัตรผ่าน bàtpàan	pass
บัตรประจำตัว bàt-bprà-jam-dtua	I.D. card
ใบขับขี่ bai-kàpkìi	driver's license
ประชาชน bprà-chaa-chon	citizen, people
โรค rôok	disease
อย่าง yàang	kind, sort, like, -ly
ดูหนัง duu-nǎng	to watch a movie
จอง jɔɔng	to reserve

Particles

Thai has many particles which can be used at the end of a sentence. These words by themselves are meaningless. However, they can change the attitude of a sentence a great deal.

The following are some common ones.

นะ (ná) is a particle commonly used at the end of a sentence in several ways.

1. It is used to make the statement softer and gentler, especially if the statement is a command.

e.g.	มานี่นะ	Come here!
	อย่านะ	Don't do it! / Please don't.

2. It is used with other verbs to imply that the speaker is persuading, suggesting or asking for agreement.

e.g.	ไปด้วยกันนะ	Let's go together. / Shall we go together?
	ดีนะ	Very well. / All right.
	คนนั้นสวยนะ	That person is beautiful, isn't she?

3. It is used with a question to imply a sense of mildness and gentleness.

e.g.	ใครนะ อยู่ที่นั่น	Who is it over there?
	ที่ไหนนะ ที่คุณไป	Where was the place that you went?

4. It is used with a question when asking someone to repeat what they said.

อะไรนะ	What? / What did you say?
ที่ไหนนะ	Where? / Where was that again?

5. It is used to express mild reproach or criticism.

e.g.   คุณนะคุณ ทำไมไม่มาหาฉัน
Oh, you, why don't you come to see me?

น่ะ (nâ) sounds similar to นะ (ná) but the tone is different and it can have either somewhat the same meaning as นะ or it can be very different.

1. It is used to express urging or insisting.

e.g.   มาน่ะ   Come! Come on, please!
ชอบน่ะ   I like it!

2. It is used as a particle to follow a word or phrase for emphasis before finishing a sentence.

e.g.   อาหารไทยน่ะ อร่อยมาก
Thai food (you know) is very delicious.
วันที่คุณมาน่ะ ผมไม่อยู่
The day you came, I wasn't here.

สิ/ สิ / สี (sì/sí/sii) Although these three are pronounced slightly different, they have the same meaning.

1. They are used as an imperative particle after a verb to suggest urgency, a request or a command. They give a stronger emphasis than นะ.

e.g.	มาสิ	Come!
	กินสิ	Eat!

2. They are used to emphasize confirmation.

e.g.	ชอบไหม	Do you like it?
	-ชอบสิ	- Sure!
	คุณจะมาไหม	Are you coming?
	-มาสิ	- Sure!

จัง (jang) is a colloquialism meaning "very much", "extremely". It is often used to express excitement or positive feelings and usually comes after a verb or adjective.

e.g.	สวยจัง	How pretty!
	คนนั้นผอมจัง	That person is extremely thin!

เลย (ləəi) is a particle that can be used by itself or combined with other words. It also has other usages in addition to being a particle.

1. เลย meaning "at all" (used after a negative).

   e.g. ไม่ชอบเลย   I don't like it at all.

      อันนี้ไม่ดีเลย   This one is not good at all.

2. เลย is used after จัง to express more excitement, pleasant feelings.

   e.g. สวยจังเลย   How pretty!

      คนนั้นผอมจังเลย That person is extremely
                   thin!

3. เลย has the meaning "so", "then", "consequently".

   e.g. วันนี้ไม่สบาย เลยไปหาหมอ
      I'm not feeling well today, so I went to see a
       doctor.
      ขี้เกียจ เลยไม่ทำงาน
      I'm lazy, so I'm not working.

จ๊ะ (já) is also a particle having the same function as ครับ and คะ, but can be used by both men and women (although women seem to use it more than men.)

1. จ๊ะ is a final particle used when asking question. Friends and people who are close to each other can use จ๊ะ instead of ครับ and คะ . It can be used when talking to children, inferiors or intimates.

	e.g.	จะไปไหนจ๊ะ	Where are you going?
		กินสิจ๊ะ	Go ahead and eat.

2. จ๊ะ is a particle placed after name, title or kin terms to address or call the attention of someone. It can be used instead of ครับ and คะ when talking to children, inferiors or intimates.

	e.g.	หนูจ๊ะ	You! (Calling a little child)
		เล็กจ๊ะ	Lek! (Calling Lek)

จ๊ะ (jâ) is also a particle having the same function as ครับ and ค่ะ.

1. จ๊ะ means 'yes', in answer to a question.

e.g.	กินข้าวหรือยัง	Have you eaten?
	–กินแล้วจ๊ะ	-Yes, I have.
	ชอบไหมจ๊ะ	Do you like it?
	–ชอบจ๊ะ	-Yes.

2. จ๊ะ is a final particle of statements used in stead of ครับ and ค่ะ when talking to children, inferiors or intimates.

e.g.	มาแล้วจ๊ะ	I've arrived.
	ดีมากจ๊ะ	Very good.

ล่ะ (lâ) is a particle used to create questions. It is also used at the end of a statement for emphasis.

e.g.	ผมสบายดี คุณล่ะ	I'm fine. And you?
	อะไรอีกล่ะ	What else? (When irritated)

หรอก/ร๊อก (rɔ̀ɔk/rɔ́k - sometimes pronouced as lɔ̀ɔk/lɔ́k) is a particle often used with statements of negation. It also makes a statement milder, less abrupt or more reassuring.

e.g.	ไม่ใช่หรอกครับ	That's not right.
	ไม่ต้องไปหรอก	That's not necessary
	ผมเองหรอกครับ	It's just me.

ซะ (sá) is a short form of เสีย. Most people these days prefer to use ซะ.

It is an imperative used after the verb to create a command.

e.g.   กินซะ   Go ahead and eat.

         ไปซะ   Go!

หรือเปล่า/รึเปล่า (rŭu-bplào/rú-bplào) is a particle used to create a yes-no question. It can sometimes be used interchangeably with ไหม/มั้ย (măi/mái) .

e.g.   จะไปหรือเปล่า Are you going?

         ชอบรึเปล่า   Do you like it?

เถอะ (tɔ̀) is a particle used as a persuasion or soft command.

e.g.   ไปเถอะ   Let's go!

         ทำเถอะ   Go ahead and do it!

เหรอ/หรือ/เรอะ (rə̌ə-/rŭu/rə̀) is a mild response to a comment or request. It is used mostly among intimates.

e.g.   เหรอครับ/ หรือครับ   Is that so?

         งั้นเรอะ   Is that it?

         ใช่หรือ   Is that right? (I doubt it.)

หน่อย normally means "a little, a little bit, a little while". When it is used at the end of a request as a particle, it makes the request milder or more polite.

> หน่อย can be replaced by ด้วย and retain the same meaning.

e.g.   ขอน้ำหน่อย (ขอน้ำด้วย)   Could you give me water?

ช่วยผมหน่อยนะ (ช่วยผมด้วยนะ) Could you help me?

The following shows how the above particles are used together.

นะครับ/ นะคะ/ นะจ๊ะ

สิครับ/ สิคะ/ สินะ

จังนะ/ จังครับ/ จังค่ะ/ จังนะครับ/ จังนะคะ

เลยนะ/ เลยนะครับ/ เลยนะคะ

จังเลย/ จังเลยนะ/ จังเลยครับ/ จังเลยค่ะ/ จังเลยนะครับ/ จังเลยนะคะ

ล่ะนะ/ ล่ะครับ/ ล่ะคะ/ ล่ะนะครับ/ ล่ะนะคะ

หรอกนะ/ หรอกครับ/ หรอกคะ/ หรอกนะครับ/ หรอกนะคะ

ซะนะ/ ซะนะครับ/ ซะนะคะ

ด้วยนะ/ ด้วยครับ/ ด้วยคะ/ ด้วยนะครับ/ ด้วยนะคะ

เถอะครับ/ เถอะคะ/ เถอะนะ/ เถอะนะครับ/ เถอะนะคะ

เหรอครับ/ เหรอคะ

หน่อยนะ/ หน่อยครับ/ หน่อยคะ/ หน่อยนะครับ/ หน่อยนะคะ

Note: Although these particles do not have any meaning in themselves, they are very important to use when expressing feelings. Consider how the attitude of the sentence changes using different particles.

"มานี" with different particles:

❑ มานี่ - "Come here!" (This statement is not very polite. The listener can feel a strong command in the speech. It is used with your friends or those who are inferior to you.)

❑ มานี่หน่อย - "Come here!" (This statement is softer. It has a sense of request.)

❑ มานี่หน่อยนะ - "Come here!" (This one is more pleasant to hear than the other two. The listener feels that you care about him/her.)

❑ มานี่หน่อยนะคะ/ครับ, มานี่ค่ะ/ครับ - "Come here!" (This is like มานี่หน่อยนะ but with a person you want to be extremely polite with, such as your teacher, your boss, adult acquaintances, etc.)

"ดี" with different particles:

❑ ดี - "Good."

❑ ดีจัง - "Very good"

❑ ดีจังเลย - "Very very good"

❑ ดีจังเลยนะ - "Very very good, isn't it?"

❑ ดีจังเลยนะครับ/นะคะ - "Very very good, isn't it?" (More polite)

ประโยค

1.   ระวังตัวนะ
        ระวังตัวนะครับ
        ระวังตัวนะคะ
        ระวังตัวด้วยนะ

2.   ผมทำอาหารเอง
        ดิฉันเรียนภาษาไทยเอง
        เขาไปเมืองไทยด้วยตัวเอง

3.   ตัวหนังสือไทยอ่านยากจัง
        ตัวหนังสือจีนเขียนยากจังเลย
        ตัวนี้เรียกว่าอะไร
        ตัวนี้เรียกว่าตัว ศ. ศาลา

4.   ผมอ่านตัวเลขไทยไม่ได้

5.   ยกตัวอย่างด้วยครับ
        ขอตัวอย่างหน่อยนะคะ
        ผมไม่เข้าใจตัวอย่างนี้เลย

6.   ผมเป็นตัวแทนจากบริษัทรถยนต์
   เขาเป็นตัวตลก

7.   ผมเคยตัวแล้ว

8.   เขายังไม่เคยชินกับที่นี่
   ผมชินแล้วล่ะครับ

9.   ขอตัวกลับก่อนนะ
   ฉันขอตัวไปห้องน้ำ

10.   ทำตัวให้ดีๆนะ
    เด็กคนนี้ทำตัวไม่ค่อยดีเลย

11.   คนไทยใช้บัตรประจำตัวประชาชน
    ผมมีโรคประจำตัว

12.   เราไม่รู้ตัวว่าเขาคิดไม่ดีกับเรา
    ผมรักคุณอย่างไม่รู้ตัว

13.   นอนหลับอย่างไม่รู้สึกตัว
    เขารู้สึกตัวแล้ว

14. ผู้หญิงคนนั้นชอบเล่นตัว
    คุณอย่าเล่นตัวเลย
    ผมไม่ชอบคนเล่นตัว

15. ห้องนี้เป็นห้องส่วนตัวของฉัน
    ของใช้ส่วนตัวอยู่ในกระเป๋า
    อันนี้เป็นของส่วนรวม ไม่ใช่ส่วนตัว

16. น้อยเสียตัวเมื่ออายุสิบเก้า

17. เดือนนี้หมดตัวแล้ว
    ผมหมดตัวจริงๆ

18. เราซื้อตั๋วไปกลับเมืองไทย
    ตั๋วใบนี้ราคาเท่าไหร่

19. ขอดูใบขับขี่คุณด้วยครับ
    ผมให้ตำรวจดูใบขับขี่

20. เราได้รับบัตรเชิญไปงานแต่งงาน
    ไม่มีบัตร ไปไม่ได้
    ผมจะไปซื้อบัตรผ่านประตู

บทสนทนา ๑

พอลกับจินดา

พอล: คุณจินดาทำงานอะไรครับ
จินดา: ผมเป็นตัวแทนขายครับ
พอล: งานยุ่งหรือเปล่าครับ
จินดา: ยุ่งมากเลย ขอตัวไปทำงานก่อนนะครับ

บทสนทนา ๒

สมศักดิ์กับจินนี่

สมศักดิ์:   คุณจินนี่พูดไทยชัดมากเลย
             เรียนภาษาไทยที่ไหนครับ
จินนี่:   เรียนที่วัดไทยในอเมริกาและก็เรียน
             ด้วยตัวเองค่ะ
สมศักดิ์:   เก่งจริงๆ เลยนะครับ ผมต้องเอาเป็น
             ตัวอย่าง ผมอยากพูดภาษาอังกฤษ
             ให้เก่งๆเหมือนอย่างที่คุณพูดไทย
จินนี่:   ไปเรียนที่เอ. ยู. เอ. สิคะ ที่นั่นมีอาจารย์
             จากต่างประเทศเยอะแยะเลย

<u>บทสนทนา ๓</u>

คิมกับสุรี

คิม: คืนนี้ไปดูหนังด้วยกันไหม
สุรี:   ไปไม่ได้หรอก หมดตัวตั้งแต่อาทิตย์ก่อนแล้ว
             ตอนนี้ไม่มีเงินติดตัวเลย
คิม: ไม่เป็นไร ผมมีตั๋วฟรีสองใบ
สุรี:   ดีจังเลย ขอบคุณมากนะ

Test 9

Match the English words with the Thai words.

_____	1. to behave	a.	ตัวอย่าง
_____	2. by oneself	b.	ทำตัว
_____	3. to get hurt	c.	ด้วยตัวเอง
_____	4. agent	d.	คนขายตัว
_____	5. to be broke	e.	ตั๋วไปกลับ
_____	6. example	f.	ส่วนตัว
_____	7. to play hard to get	g.	ตัวเลข
_____	8. to be aware	h.	ตัวแทน
_____	9. to excuse oneself	i.	ตั๋วเที่ยวเดียว
_____	10. round-trip ticket	j.	เจ็บตัว
_____	11. to get into the habit of	k.	เคยตัว
_____	12. numeral figure	l.	รู้ตัว
_____	13. one-way ticket	m.	ตัวหนังสือ
_____	14. letter of the alphabet	n.	ขอตัว
_____	15. personal	o.	เสียตัว
		p.	หมดตัว
		q.	ตัว
		r.	เล่นตัว

Translate the following into English.

1.   อยู่ที่นี่   ทำตัวให้ดีนะ

_____

2.   อย่าเล่นตัวสิ

_____

3.   คุณเล่นเทนนิสเก่งจังเลย

_____

4.   ขอซื้อตั๋วไปกลับสองใบครับ

_____

5.   ทำอาหารไทยกันเถอะ

_____

Lesson 10
บทที่ ๑๐

บทที่ ๑๐

คำศัพท์	Vocabulary
สำหรับ sǎmràp	for
เพื่อ pûa	for, in order to
นานเท่าไหร่ naantâo-rài	how long
ตั้งแต่เมื่อไหร่ dtâng-dtɛ̀ɛ-mûa-rài	since when
ด้วย dûai	with, by
ภายใน paai-nai	within
ก่อน gɔ̀ɔn	before
หลัง lǎng	after
(ใน) เร็วๆนี้ (nai) reo-reo-níi	soon
เท่านั้น/เฉพาะ tâo-nán/chà-pɔ́	only
เหมาะสำหรับ mɔ̀-sǎmràp	good for
เพิ่ง pə̂ng	just, just now
ต้น dtôn	the beginning of
ปลาย/สิ้น bplaai/sîn	the end of
ต้นปี dtôn-bpii	beginning of the year
ปลายปี/สิ้นปี bplaai-bpii/sîn-bpii	end of the year
ต้นเดือน dtôndɨan	beginning of the month
ปลายเดือน/สิ้นเดือน	end of the month
bplaai-dɨan/sîndɨan	
ทั้ง táng	all
ทั้งวัน tâng-wan	all day
ทั้งคืน tâng-kɨɨn	all night
ทั้งปี tâng-bpii	all year

เว้น wén	to skip over
วันเว้นวัน wanwénwan	every other day
วันหยุดราชการ	official holiday
wan-yùt-râatchá-gaan	
ยกเว้น/นอกจาก yók-wén/nɔ̂ɔkjàak	except
เงินเดือน ngən-dɯan	monthly salary
มนุษย์ má-nút	human
สังคม sǎngkom	society
ประสบการณ์ bprà-sòpgaan	experience
วิชา wí-chaa	subject
เลข/คณิตศาสตร์ lêek/ká-nítsàat	math
วิทยาศาสตร์ wíttá-yaatsàat	science
ประวัติศาสตร์ bprà-wàtsàat	history
สังคมศึกษา sǎngkomsɯ̀ksǎa	social studies
วรรณคดี wanná-ká-dii	literature
ภาษาต่างประเทศ	foreign language
paa-sǎa-dtàang-bprà-têet	
ตะเกียบ dtà-gìap	chopsticks
มีด mîit	knife
ช้อน chɔ́ɔn	spoon
ส้อม sɔ̂m	fork
เก็บเงิน gèp-ngən	to save money
เกิด gə̀ət	to be born
สู้ sûu	to fight
ขอให้ kɔ̌ɔ-hâi	(I) wish you...
สักครู่ sàkkrûu	one moment
สุขภาพ sùkkà-pâap	health
สาย sǎai	line

Name of the Twelve Cyclical Years

ปีชวด/ปีหนู
    bpii-chûat/bpii-nǔu

Year of the Mouse

ปีฉลู/ปีวัว
    bpii-chà-lǔu/bpii-wua

Year of the Ox

ปีขาล/ปีเสือ
    bpii-kǎan/bpii-sǔa

Year of the Tiger

ปีเถาะ/ปีกระต่าย
    bpii-tò/bpii-grà-dtàai

Year of the Rabbit

ปีมะโรง/ปีงูใหญ่
    bpii-má-roong/bpii-nguu-yài

Year of the Dragon

ปีมะเส็ง/ปีงูเล็ก
    bpii-má-sěng/bpii-nguu-lék

Year of the Snake

ปีมะเมีย/ปีม้า
    bpii-má-mia/bpii-máa

Year of the Horse

ปีมะแม/ปีแพะ
    bpii-má-mɛɛ/bpii-pέ

Year of the Goat

ปีวอก/ปีลิง
    bpii-wɔ̂ɔk/bpii-ling

Year of the Monkey

ปีระกา/ปีไก่
    bpii-rá-gaa/bpii-gài

Year of the Chicken

ปีจอ/ปีหมา
    bpii-jɔɔ/bpii-mǎa

Year of the Dog

ปีกุน/ปีหมู
    bpii-gun/bpii-mǔu

Year of the Pig

WORDS FROM ENGLISH

There are quite a few English words in modern Thai. However, they are given a Thai pronunciation. Here are some common English words and how Thai people say them.

acre	เอเคอร์	ee-kɔ̂ɔ
AIDS	เอดส์	èet, èes
agent	เอเย่นต์	èe-yên
album	อัลบัม	a-lá-bâm
American football	อเมริกันฟุตบอล	à-mee-rí-gan fútbɔɔn
apartment	อาพาร์ตเมนต์	aa-páatmént
bank	แบงค์	béng
bar	บาร์	baa
bartender	บาร์เทนเดอร์	baa-tendɔ̂ɔ
basketball	บาสเกตบอล	báatsàgétbɔɔn
battery	แบตเตอรี่	bèttəərîi
beer	เบียร์	bia
bellboy	บ๋อย	bɔ̌i
Bible	ไบเบิล	bai-bân
bonus	โบนัส	boo-nát, boo-nás
boutique	บูติก	buu-dtìk
bowling	โบลิ่ง	boo-lîng
brake	เบรค	brèek
brandy	บรั่นดี	bà-ràndii
bus	บัส	bát, bás

care (v.)	แคร์	kɛɛ
cashier	แคชเชียร์	kétchia
catalogue	แคตาลอก	két-dtaa-lɔ́k
cement	ซีเมนต์	sii-ment
check-in	เช็คอิน	chék-in
check-out	เช็คเอาท์	chék-áo
chocolate	ชอกโกแลต	chɔ́kgo-lét
classic	คลาสสิค	klátsìk
club	คลับ	klàp
clutch	คลัตช์	klát
cocktail	คอกเทล	kɔ́kteo
communist	คอมมิวนิสต์	kɔmmiu-nít
computer	คอมพิวเตอร์	kɔmpíu-dtɔ̂ə
concrete (n.)	คอนกรีต	kɔngrìit
contact lens	คอนแทคเลนส์	kɔntɛ̀kleen
copy	กอปปี้	gɔ́p-bpî
coupon	คูปอง	kuu-bpɔɔng
dictionary	ดิก	dìk
disco	ดิสโก้	dítsà-gôo
elevator, lift	ลิฟท์	líp
email	อีเมล์	ii-mee
farm	ฟาร์ม	faam
fashion	แฟชั่น	fɛɛ-chân
fax	แฟกซ์	fɛ̀k, fɛ̀ks
film	ฟิล์ม	fiim
fit (v.)	ฟิต	fít
foot (measurement)	ฟุต	fút

football	ฟุตบอล	fútbɔɔn
free	ฟรี	frii
gas	แกส, กาซ	gɛ́ɛt, gáas
gear	เกียร์	gia
gel	เจล	jeo
golf	กอล์ฟ	gɔ́ɔp
gram	กรัม	gram
graph	กราฟ	gráap
guide	ไกด์	gái
guitar	กีตาร์	gii-dtâa
hello (on the phone)	ฮัลโหล	hanlǒo
hotel	โฮเต็ล	hoo-dten
ice cream	ไอสครีม, ไอติม	ái-sà-kriim, ai-dtim
internet	อินเตอร์เน็ท	intəə-nèt
jelly	เยลลี่	yenɺii
kaki	กากี	gaa-gii
kilo	กิโล	gì-loo
laser	เลเซอร์	lee-sɔ̂ə
lecture	เลคเชอร์	lékchɔ̂ə
lobby	ลอบบี้	lɔ́pɓii
locker	ลอคเกอร์	lɔ́kgɔ̂ə
meter (length)	เมตร	méet
meter (scale)	มีเตอร์	mít-dtɔ̂ə
mile	ไมล์	maai
motorcycle	มอเตอร์ไซ	mɔɔ-dtəə-sai
necktie	เนคไท, ไท	néktai, tái

net	เน็ต, เน็ท	nét
nightclub	ไนท์คลับ	nái-klàp
nylon	ไนลอน	nai-lôn
office	ออฟฟีส	ว́pfít, ว́pfís
okay	โอเค	oo-kee
on-line	ออนไลน์	ɔɔnlaai
over-time	โอเวอร์ไทม์, โอที	oo-wɔ̂ɔ-taam, oo-tii
party	ปาร์ตี้	bpaa-dtîi
physics	ฟิสิกส์	fí-sìk
percent	เปอร์เซนต์	bpɔɔ-sen
plastic	พลาสติก	pláatsà-dtìk
poster	โปสเตอร์	bpótsà-tɔ̂ɔ
program	โปรแกรม	bproo-grɛɛm
romantic	โรแมนติก	roo-mɛɛn-dtìk
room service	รูมเซอร์วิส	ruumsɔɔ-wít
sandwich	แซนวิช	sɛɛnwít
safe (n.)	เซฟ	séep
serious	ซีเรียส	sii-rìat
service	เซอร์วิส	sɔɔ-wít
sex	เซกซ์	sék, séks
sexy	เซกซี่	séksîi
shock	ชอค	chɔ́k
shopping	ชอปปิ้ง	chɔ́p bpîŋ
skate	สเกต	sà-gét
sketch	สเกตช์	sà-gét
ski	สกี	sà-gii

smart	สมาร์ท	sà-máat
soda	โซดา	soo-daa
soup	ซุป	súp
spaghetti	สปาเก็ตตี้	sà-bpaa-gét-dtîi
stamp	สแตมป์	sà-dtɛm
staple	สแตปเปิล	sà-dtee-bpə̂n
steak	สะเต๊ก	sà-dtéek
stereo	สเตริโอ	sà-dtee-rí-oo
studio	สตูดิโอ	sà-dtuu-dì-oo
style	สไตล์	sà-dtaai
sure	ชัวร์	chua
taxi	แทกซี่	téksîi
technique	เทคนิค	téknìk
technology	เทคโนโลยี	téknoo-loo-yîi
telex	เทเลกซ์	tee-lèk, tee-lèks
tennis	เทนนิส	tenník, tenník
tent	เต้นท์	dtén
TV	ทีวี	tii-wii
video	วีดีโอ	wii-dii-oo
view	วิว	wiu
violin	ไวโอลิน	wai-oo-lin
volleyball	วอลเลย์บอล	wɔnlêebɔɔn
whisky	วิสกี้	wítsà-gîi
wine	ไวน์	wain
X-ray	เอกซ์เรย์	éksà-ree

ประโยค

1.   กระเป๋าใบนี้สำหรับคุณ = กระเป๋าใบนี้ให้คุณ

2.   คุณทำเพื่อใคร   -เพื่อคุณนะสิ
      เขาทำงานเพื่อใคร   -เพื่อครอบครัว
      เราสู้เพื่อประเทศ

3.   คุณมาอเมริกาเพื่ออะไร   -เพื่อหาเงิน
      กินเพื่ออยู่ ไม่ใช่อยู่เพื่อกิน

4.   เขาเรียนภาษาไทยนานเท่าไหร่ -สองปี
      คุณอยู่ที่นี่นานเท่าไหร่แล้ว   -เกือบสิบปีแล้ว

5.   เขาเรียนภาษาไทยตั้งแต่เมื่อไหร่
      -ตั้งแต่สองปีที่แล้ว
      คุณอยู่ที่นี่ตั้งแต่เมื่อไหร่
      -ตั้งแต่สิบปีที่แล้ว

6.   เขียนจดหมายด้วยปากกาเต็ม
      เรียนภาษาไทยด้วยตัวเอง
      คนไทยกินอาหารด้วยช้อนกับส้อม
      คนญี่ปุ่นกินอาหารด้วยตะเกียบ

7.   คุณจะกลับมาเมื่อไหร่   – ภายในพรุ่งนี้
     งานจะเสร็จกี่โมง   – ภายในบ่ายโมง

8.   เราจะไปสนามบินกี่โมง   – ก่อนเที่ยง
     เขาจะมาถึงเมื่อไหร่   – หลังห้าโมงเย็น

9.   ดิฉันจะไปเมืองไทยเร็วๆนี้
     เราจะพบกันในเร็วๆนี้

10. วันอาทิตย์เท่านั้น
     = เฉพาะวันอาทิตย์
     ผมไปวัดวันอาทิตย์เท่านั้น
     = ผมไปวัดเฉพาะวันอาทิตย์

11. หนังสือเล่มนี้เหมาะสำหรับเด็ก
     น้ำนี้ไม่เหมาะสำหรับดื่ม

12. คุณมาถึงเมื่อไหร่   – เพิ่งมา
     เขาเพิ่งแต่งงาน
     อย่าเพิ่งไป!

13. ต้นเดือนหน้าจะไปเที่ยวญี่ปุ่น
     เขามาอยู่อเมริกาตั้งแต่ต้นปีนี้

14. เราแต่งงานปลายปีที่แล้ว
เงินเดือนออกตอนสิ้นเดือน

15. เขาทำงานทั้งวัน
ปีที่แล้วฝนตกทั้งปี

16. ผมทำงานทุกวัน เว้นวันอาทิตย์
เปิดบริการทุกวัน เว้นวันหยุดราชการ
เรามาที่นี่วันเว้นวัน
ผมดื่มทุกอย่างยกเว้นกาแฟ

17. สังคมไทยที่นี่ใหญ่มาก
มนุษย์เป็นสัตว์สังคม

18. เขามีประสบการณ์ที่ญี่ปุ่น
เด็กคนนี้มีประสบการณ์มาก

19. คุณเกิดปีอะไร
–เกิดปีไก่ (เกิดปีระกา)

20. ขอให้หายเร็วๆ
ขอให้คุณมีเงินเยอะๆ
ขอให้มีสุขภาพดี

บทสนทนา ๑

สุขใจกับแดน (พูดโทรศัพท์)

แดน: ฮัลโหล คุณสมชายอยู่ไหมครับ
สุขใจ: คุณสมชายไม่อยู่ค่ะ ใครโทรมาคะ
แดน: ผมแดนพูดครับ
สุขใจ: พรุ่งนี้โทรมาใหม่นะคะ วันนี้คุณสมชาย
            ไม่กลับออฟฟิสแล้วค่ะ
แดน: เหรอครับ ขอบคุณมากครับ

บทสนทนา ๒

ศิริกับซู (พูดโทรศัพท์)

ศิริ:   สวัสดีครับ ศิริพูดครับ
ซู:   ฮัลโหล ขอสายกับคุณเล็กด้วยค่ะ
ศิริ:   รอสักครู่นะครับ คุณเล็กติดสายอีก
            เครื่องหนึ่งอยู่ครับ
ซู:   ไม่เป็นไรค่ะ เดี๋ยวจะโทรมาใหม่

<u>บทสนทนา ๓</u>

รอนกับปิติ

ปิติ:   ตอนเป็นนักเรียน คุณชอบวิชาอะไรมากที่สุด

รอน: ชอบวิชาวิทยาศาสตร์และก็วิชาเลข
          คุณปิติล่ะครับ

ปิติ:   ผมชอบวิชาภาษาอังกฤษ แต่เรียนไม่ค่อยเก่ง
          ตอนนี้คุณทำงานอะไรครับ

รอน: ผมเป็นหมอครับ ทำงานที่โรงพยาบาล
          ในอเมริกา แล้วคุณทำงานที่ไหนครับ

ปิติ:   ผมทำงานกับบริษัทฝรั่งเศส

รอน: คุณชอบงานของคุณหรือเปล่า

ปิติ:   ชอบครับ งานนี้ต้องรู้ภาษาต่างประเทศมาก
          ผมก็เลยได้ใช้วิชาที่เรียนมา
          คุณรอนชอบเป็นหมอไหมครับ

รอน: ไม่ค่อยชอบหรอกครับ ถึงแม้เงินจะดี
          แต่ต้องทำงานหนักมาก ไม่ค่อยมีเวลาให้ครอบครัว

บทสนทนา ๔

โสภณกับแรนดี้

โสภณ:　คุณแรนดี้ทำงานที่นี่ตั้งแต่เมื่อไหร่ครับ

แรนดี้:　ประมาณสามปีแล้ว คุณล่ะครับ

โสภณ:　ผมเพิ่งจะเริ่มทำงานต้นปีนี้

แรนดี้:　คุณทำงานหนักจังเลยนะครับ

โสภณ:　ผมกำลังเก็บเงินเพื่อซื้อบ้านครับ
　　　　แล้วก็คิดว่าจะแต่งงาน

แรนดี้:　คุณมีแฟนแล้วหรือครับ

โสภณ:　มีแล้วครับ ชื่ออ้อย อายุน้อยกว่าผมสองปี
　　　　ผมเกิดปีเถาะ อ้อยเกิดปีมะเส็ง

แรนดี้:　ขอให้โชคดีนะครับ

Test 10

Match the English words with the Thai words.

_____	1. before	a.	ต้นปี
_____	2. every other day	b.	วิชา
_____	3. to save money	c.	เกิด
_____	4. only	d.	สังคม
_____	5. to be born	e.	สาย
_____	6. end of the month	f.	หลัง
_____	7. all year	g.	ปลายเดือน
_____	8. experience	h.	ภายใน
_____	9. to fight	i.	วันเว้นวัน
_____	10. line	j.	เท่านั้น
_____	11. human	k.	ทั้งปี
_____	12. subject	l.	มนุษย์
_____	13. to except	m.	สู้
_____	14. society	n.	ก่อน
_____	15. within	o.	เก็บเงิน
		p.	วันหยุดราชการ
		q.	ประสบการณ์
		r.	ยกเว้น

Translate the following into English.

1. คุณทำงานที่บริษัทนี้นานเท่าไหร่แล้ว
    –ประมาณห้าปีครึ่ง

    _____

2. สมชายไปทำงานเฉพาะวันจันทร์และวันอังคาร

    _____

3. เขาเกิดปีอะไร   –ปีมะแม

    _____

4. ผมจะกลับเมืองไทยต้นปีหน้า

    _____

5. ฉันไม่เหมาะสำหรับคุณ

    _____

English
Translation

English Translation

Lesson 1

Sentences (page 20)

1. Come this way.
   Go that way.
2. The car is on the left.
   The house is on the right.
3. Which way is the hotel? - To the right.
   Which way is the Thai restaurant? - Over there.
4. The book is on the right.
   The pen is on the left.
   The bank is in front (of you).
   The airport is behind (you).
5. Where is the pencil?   - On the left.
   Where is the school?   - On the right.
6. Send the letter by airmail.
   Come by boat.
7. It's too spicy.
   Thai food is too spicy.
   I think Thai food is too spicy.
8. Thailand has four regions: the North, the Northeast, the Central and the South.
9. Which region do you come from?   - From the North.
   Which region does he come from?   - From the Northeast.
10. Thailand has 76 provinces.
11. Which province do you come from?   - From Bangkok.
    Which province does he come from?   - From Chiangrai.
12. Bangkok has 38 districts.
    Phuket has 3 districts.
13. Which district do you live in?   - I live in the central district.
14. Thailand has three seasons: hot season, rainy season and cold season.

15. How many seasons are there in Japan?
    - There are 4 seasons: spring, summer, autumn and winter.
16. I like Thai traditions very much.
    He loves Thai culture.
17. What day is today? - Today is Songkran Day.
18. Thai people make merit on New Year's Day.
19. In Thailand, rice farming is done in the rainy season.
20. We will go to Loy Kratong Day Festival.

Conversation (page 23)

Conversation 1

Mary:	Excuse me. Where is the bank?
Somchai:	It's on the left.
Mary:	Thank you.
Somchai:	You're welcome.

Conversation 2

Mali:	John, what country are you from?
John:	I'm from Nevada, America. What province are you from, Mali?
Mali:	From Chiangmai. But I'm working in Bangkok. How long will you be in Thailand?
John:	About two weeks. I will return to America on 15th.

Conversation 3

Lek:	Do you like Thailand?
Akiko:	Very much. I like Thai people and Thai food, but I think that the weather is too hot.
Lek:	But in the North and the Northeast we have a cold season.
Akiko:	Is that right? I've never been to that area.

Conversation 4

Mark:	Today is Songkran Day. Where are you going to celebrate?
Giti:	I will go to the temple because they are having a big festival there.
Mark:	Can I go with you?
Giti:	Yes. The festival at the temple is fun every year.
Mark:	When are you going?
Giti:	On Sunday. At noon. I will pick you up then.

Lesson 2

Sentences (page 37)

1. The Dusit Hotel is on the left.
2. Go straight, then turn right.
3. Turn right first, then turn left.
4. The train station is in front (of you).
5. The weather is very hot outside.
6. I live upstairs.
7. Go straight ahead.
8. The bus stop is at the intersection.
9. Stop here.
10. I have only a hundred baht bill. Do you have change?
11. I don't have change.
12. I will arrive in Thailand tomorrow.
13. I will pick up my friend at the airport.
14. He goes shopping at a department store.
15. We go to the train station by taxi.
16. The American Embassy is on Wireless Road.
17. I work at the Ministry of Foreign Affairs.
18. I came to pick up my girlfriend at the bus terminal.
19. There are not many public telephones in Bangkok.
20. I want to go to the Emerald Buddha Temple.

Conversation (page 39)

Conversation 1

Taxi Driver:	Where are you going?
Tony:	To the Sukhumvit Crown Hotel.
Taxi Driver:	Which Soi is it on?
Tony:	It's on Sukhumvit 8. ....
	Turn left. Stop here. How much is it?
Taxi Driver:	It's fifty baht.
Tony:	I only have a hundred (baht) bill. Do you have change?
Taxi Driver:	No. I can exchange at the restaurant.
Tony:	That's O.K. You don't have to give me the change.
Taxi Driver:	Thank you. Good luck.

Conversation 2

Noi:	When will you return to America?
David:	In two days.
Noi:	I want to see you off. What time will you go to the airport?
David:	I will arrive at the airport at nine p.m. The plane leaves at eleven.
Noi:	O.K. See you at the airport at nine.

Conversation 3

Tom:	Excuse me. Where is the Malasian Embassy?
Dang:	Go straight, turn left at the intersection, then turn right. The embassy is on the right.
Tom:	Thank you very much.
Dang:	You're welcome.

Lesson 3

Sentences (page 49)

1. Who gives the students homework?
   - The teacher gives students homework.
   Who did you give the present to?
   - I gave the present to my girlfriend.
2. Who teaches you Thai?
   - He teaches me Thai.
   Who do you teach Thai to?
   - I teach Thai to him.
3. Who let/made you go?   - He let/made me go.
   Who did you let/ make go?   - I let/made him go.
4. Who wants you to go?   - He wants me to go.
   Who do you want to go?   - I want him to go.
5. Who will let/make you go?   - He will let/make me go.
   Who will you let/make go?   - I will let/make him go.
6. Shall I take a picture for you?
   Shall we write a letter for you?
7. Wipe it clean.
   Correct it.
   Please write nicely.
8. Turn off the light (for me).
   Call a taxi (for me).
   Please turn the fan on (for me).
9. We rent a house in America.
10 There is a house for rent here.
11. He borrowed money from me.
    I loaned him money.
12. I encouraged my friends.
13. Come, by all means!
    I will go to Thailand by all means/absolutely.
14. I interviewed the teacher.
    I was interviewed on T.V.

15. He promised me. = He gave me a promise.
16. We have a good service. = We give good service.
17. He will mail the letter for me.
18. I received a birthday present.
19. Yesterday I opened an account at the bank.
20. You helped me make food.

Conversation (page 52)

Conversation 1

Suda: You speak Thai very well.
Tim: Not so well yet. I can't listen very well.
Suda: Who taught you Thai?
Tim: A Thai teacher in America taught me Thai.
Suda: Can you read and write?
Tim: A little bit. I can read slowly. Can you teach me Thai?
Suda: I want to but I don't have time. I will tell my friend for you.
Tim: Thank you. I want to be able to read Thai well.

Conversation 2

Ann: What is your work phone number?
Seri: It's 726-5921.
Ann: Can I have your home phone number?
Seri: It's 654-0987

Conversation 3

Jane: Did you give me your address?
Mali: Not yet.
Jane: What is your house number?
Mali: It's 390 Danmuen Road, Muang District, Ubon Province

Jane: Do you know your zip code?
Mali: It's 34000.
Jane: Thank you very much.

Lesson 4

Sentences (page 64)

1. I have no feeling.
2. We have hope.
3. The Japanese love cleanliness.
4. I feel very excited.
5. In Thailand, the medical service is not so good yet.
6. America spends a lot of money on military affairs.
7. Now the economy in Thailand is not good.
8. We should emphasize education.
9. He is not of any importance.
10. I will try to succeed.
11. Where there is effort, there is success.
12. This table is two metres wide.
13. This road is ten miles long.
14. What do we have to eat?
    What things will you buy?
15. You should learn Thai.
    You must learn Thai.
16. What would you like to drink?   - Anything will do.
17. Where do you want to go?   - Anywhere will do.
18. Anybody will do.
    Any way will do.
    Whenever will do.
19. You can go with anybody.
    You can go however you like.
    You can go whenever you like.
20. Do you have money?   - Some.
    Do you like western food?   - I like some.

Conversation (page 66)

Conversation 1

Julie:	I want to buy land to do business in Thailand.
Somjai:	You are not a Thai. You can't buy.
Julie:	Why not?
Somjai:	Thai law doesn't allow foreigners to buy land.
Julie:	That's not fair!

Conversation 2

Tanaka:	How is the education in Thailand?
Yupa:	Not so good. There are still a lot of students that don't go to school.
Tanaka:	I think that the economy in Thailand is good.
Yupa:	Yes, but the governement does not pay much attention in education. There are a lot of poor people who don't go to school. How is it in Japan?
Tanaka:	I think it's good. But I want it to be better.

Conversation 3

Pichai:	Now I am having a problem at home.
Jim:	What problem?
Pichai:	My father is sick. He hasn't been working for two months.
Jim:	You should take him to see a doctor.
Pichai:	I want to, but I have have no money at this point.
Jim:	I can loan you some.
Pichai	Really? Thank you very much.

Lesson 5

Sentences (page 78)

1. There are no parking spots.
2. I will go to the office.
3. America has a lot of places to visit.
4. This mattress is wet.
5. This house has some empty space.
6. I will give you my address.
7. I know that he will come.
8. I dreamed that I went to Thailand.
9. He promised that he would come (to see me).
10. What does 'telephone' mean?
11. How do you read this?
12. What is this called in Thai?
13. This restaurant is cheap.
14. He doesn't speak Thai very correctly.
15. It didn't hit the target.
16. He doesn't seem to get along with me.
17. My younger brother/sister was hit by Mother.
18. He was bitten by a snake.
19. Don't go to bed late.
20. No entry!

Conversation (page 80)

Conversation 1

Wilai:	Please give me your address in America.
Linda:	Sure. This is my name card. There is the address and telephone number.
Wilai:	Where are you staying in Thailand?
Linda:	I'm staying with my friend in Bangkok.

Conversation 2

Laura:	How is this read?
Sopa:	It is 'gum-paa-pan'.
Laura:	What does it mean?
Sopa:	It means 'February'.
	What is this called in English.
Laura:	It is 'television'. It means 'too-rá-tát'.

Conversation 3

Suri:	Where did you buy that bag?
Don:	In Hong Kong.
Suri:	Excuse me. How much is it?
Don:	About three hundred baht.
Suri.	Very cheap.
Don:	Right. I like this bag very much.
	The price wasn't expensive, but it works well.

Lesson 6

Sentences (page 93)

ใจ

1. He is generous./He is a generous person.
2. He is not narrow-minded./He is not a narrowed minded person.
3. I like calm people.
4. Calm down. Don't be impatient.
5. You are very mean.
6. Today I feel good.
7. I'm very proud of you.
8. He is not faithful to his lover.
9. He is not very satisfied.
10. I feel sorry for you.

11. He puts a lot of attention to his work.
12. I'm not interested.
13. This person pleases others well.
14. I cannot decide.
15. I don't want to bother you.
16. It's up to you.
17. He hurt my feeling.
18. I'm really worried.
19. Mr. Somchai already changed his mind.
20. I can't breath.

1. He is shy./He is a shy person.
2. He is forgetful./He is a forgetful person.
3. He is not cheating./He is a not a cheating person.
4. I don't like stingy people.
5. You complain a lot.
6. He is a drunkard
7. He is a cigarette addict.
8. I have a boyfriend who is an alcohol addict.
9. I am sensitive to cold weather
10. He is sensitive to hot weather.
11. I'm not an unhealthy person.
12. He does not believe in you. He is very suspicious.
13. I am a sympathetic person.
14. This person is very jealous.
15. We don't like cowards.
16. I'm a playful man.
17. My girlfriend is so demanding.
18. She has a very jealous husband
19. That person is very boastful.
20. I don't like him because he likes to lie.

น่า

1. This candy looks tasty.
2. This glass of beer looks tasty.
3. He is cute./He is a cute person.
4. This town is not livable.
5. This bag is worth buying.
6. This movie is not worth watching.
7. This book is really worth reading.
8. The Thai language is worth trying.
9. I have something to think about.
10. He said something unpleasant (to listen to).
11. Unbelievable!
12. That's really scary.
13. He is a very annoying person.
14. This book is boring, not interesting at all.
15. This child is very pitiful.
16. Too bad that you couldn't come.
17. There is something suspicious (here).
18. He is a very respectful person.
19. He is not reliable.
20. This child is very cute.

Conversation (page 99)

Conversation 1

Jim:	What kind of people do you like?
Yupa:	I like gentle and kind people. And you?
	What kind of people do you like?
Jim:	I like cheerful and generous people.
Yupa:	I think that you are nice and very polite.
Jim:	Thank you. I also think that you are neat and nice.

Conversation 2

James:	What kind of person do you think he is?
Nit:	I think he is a little bit cheap. What do you think?
James:	I don't know. Do you like him?
Nit:	So-so. I don't know him well yet.

Conversation 3

Sam:	This book is very worth reading.
Gai:	What is it about?
Sam:	About the problems of the world economy.
Gai:	Interesting. Are you going to buy it?
Sam:	I think so.
Gai:	How much is it?
Sam:	Two hundred and fifty baht.
Gai:	I think it's too expensive.
Sam:	Will you buy it?
Gai:	I don't want to buy it right now. Can I read it with you?
Sam:	Sure! Don't worry.
Gai:	Thank you very much.

Lesson 7

Senten˜es (page 115)

1. What's your (official) name?
   - -My (official) name is Mana.
   - -My name is David.
2. Do you have a nickname?
   - -Yes. It's 'Lek'.
3. What is your last name?
   - -My last name is Pira.
4. Please sign your name.
5. This is fake, not a real thing.
6. Children like toys.
7. Give me the menu.
8. Check the bill!
9. Give me toothpicks.
10. Noi cried.
11. Gai laughed.
12. He already forgot about you.
13. Nok lost the money.
14. I couldn't find you.
15. I agree./I agree with you.
16. I'm really hungry.
17. Are you thirsty?   -Yes.
18. Are you full?   -Yes.
19. I want to have a lot of money.
20. There are a lot of people.

Conversation (page 117)

Conversation 1

Ken:	Hello. What's your name?
Nut:	My name is Nut.
Ken:	Is 'Nut' your official name or your nickname?
Nut:	It's my nickname. My official name is Suchada. What's your name?
Ken:	My name is Ken. I don't have a nickname. What is your last name?
Nut:	My last name is Sanmuang.

Conversation 2

Winai:	What would you like to order today?
Michael:	I want to have Tom Yum Gung and Somtam. And you?
Winai:	I want to have Padtai. Are you going to have some dessert?
Michael:	Yes. I want to have sticky rice with mango.

Conversation 3

Joe:	Mai, why are you crying?
Mai:	I lost my purse.
Joe:	Where did you lose it?
Mai:	I think at the market. This morning there were a lot of people.
Joe:	I'm sorry. That's too bad. Be careful next time.

Lesson 8

Sentences (page 135)

1. I have relatives in America.
2. I miss my parents.
3. Gai and Dang are cousins.
4. This is my nephew.
5. Noi is still single.
6. David is a widower.
7. My father-in-law is very kind.
8. Daughters-in-law and mothers-in-law don't like each other.
9. We have a 'farang' brother-in-law.
10. He will remarry.
11. Tomorrow I will go to my friend's wedding.
12. Ann will be a bridesmaid.
13. Ms. Wilai already divorced her husband.
14. The ceremony will be Thai style.
15. Monks do the ceremony for us.
16. Christians believe in God.
17. They get married in the church.
18. What religion are you?
    -I am Christian.
19. He doesn't have a religion.
20. Most Thai people are Buddhist.

Conversation (page 137)

Conversation 1

Pracha:	Excuse me. Are you married, Bill?
Bill:	Yes. My wife is Thai.
Pracha:	Do you have relatives in Thailand?
Bill:	No. Only my wife and two children.
Pracha:	What religion are you?
Bill:	I'm Christian, but my family here are Buddhist.

Conversation 2

Charlie:	Today I'm going to a wedding.
Tani:	Whose wedding is it?
Charlie:	Lek and Bunchu, her boy friend.
Tani:	Where do they have the ceremony?
Charlie:	At home in the morning. At night at the Dusit Hotel.

Conversation 3

Jack:	Dang, do you like Somchai and his friends?
Dang:	I like them very much. I think they are very nice. What do you think, Jack?
Jack:	I don't know. I don't know them very well.
Dang:	I like Mr. Somchai the best. I have worked with him for many years. I think you will also like him.

Lesson 9

Sentences (page 154)

1. Take care of yourself.
2. I cook by myself.
   I study Thai by myself.
   He goes to Thailand by himself.
3. The Thai alphabet is pretty hard to read.
   Chinese characters are pretty hard to write.
   What is this letter called?   -It's called 'sɔ̌ɔ sǎa-laa'.
4. I can't read Thai numbers.
5. Please give me an example.
   May I have an example?
   I don't understand this example.
6. I am an agent for a car company.
   He is a comedian.
7. I'm used to that habit.
8. He isn't used to this place.
   I'm used to it.
9. I want to excuse myself to leave.
   I want to excuse myself to go to the bathroom.
10. Behave yourself.
    This child doesn't behave himself well.
11. Thai people use citizen I.D. cards.
    I have a chronic disease.
12. We weren't aware that he doesn't think well of us.
    I fell in love with you without knowing it.
13. I fell asleep without knowing it.
    He is already conscious.
14. That woman likes to play hard to get.
    Don't play hard to get.
    I don't like people who play hard to get.

15. This is my private room.
    My personal things are in the bag.
    This one is public, not private.
16. Noi lost her virginity at age nineteen.
17. This month I'm already broke.
    I'm really broke.
18. We bought a round trip ticket to Thailand.
    How much is this ticket?
19. May I look at your driver's license?
    I showed my driver's license to the police.
20. We received a wedding invitation card.
    I don't have a ticket. I can't go.
    I will buy a door ticket.

Conversation (page 157)

Conversation 1

Paul:	Jinda, what kind of work do you do?.
Jinda:	I am a sales rep.
Paul:	Are you busy with your work?
Jinda:	Very busy. Excuse me. I have to go to work.

Conversation 2

Somsak:	Jinny, you can speak Thai very clearly. Where did you study Thai?
Jinny:	I studied at the Thai temple in America and I also study by myself.
Somsak	You are doing very well. I would like to follow your example. I want to speak English well like the way you speak Thai.
Jinny:	You can go to A.U.A. to study. There are a lot of teachers from overseas there.

Conversation 3

Kim:	Tonight let's go to a movie.
Suri:	I can't go. I've been broke since last week. Now I have no money at all.
Kim:	No problem. I have two free tickets.
Suri:	That's good. Thanks a lot.

Lesson 10

Sentences (page 171)

1. This bag is for you.
2. Who do you work for?   -For you!
   Who does he work for?   -For his family.
   We fight for the country.
3. What did you come to America for?   -For money.
   We eat to live, not live to eat.
4. How long has he been studying Thai?   -Two years.
   How long have you been living here?   -Almost ten years.
5. Since when has he been learning Thai?   -Since two years ago.
   Since when did you start living here?   -Since ten years ago.
6. I'm writing the letter with a black pen.
   I study Thai by myself.
   Thai people eat with spoon and fork.
   The Japanese eat with chopsticks.
7. When will you be back?   -By tomorrow.
   When will the work be over?   -By one o'clock.
8. What time will we go to the airport?   -Before noon.
   When will he arrive?   -After five o'clock.
9. I will go to Thailand soon.
   We will see each other soon.
10. On Sunday only.
    I go to the temple only on Sunday.
11. This book is good for children.
    This water is not good for drinking.
12. When did you arrive?   -Just now.
    He just got married.
    Don't go yet!
13. I will take a trip to Japan the beginning of next month.
    He has been in America since the beginning of this year.

14. We got married at the end of last year.
Our salary comes at the end of the month.
15. He works all day.
Last year it rained all year long.
16. I work everyday, except Sunday.
(We) open for service everyday, except official holidays.
We come here every other day.
I drink everything, except coffee.
17. The Thai community here is very big.
Human is a social animal.
18. He has experience living in Japan.
This child has a lot of experience.
19. Which year were you born?   -Year of the Chicken.
20. I wish you a quick recovery.
I wish you a lot of money.
I wish you good health.

Conversation (page 174)

Conversation 1

Dan: Hello! Is Mr. Somchai there?
Sukjai: Mr. Somchai is not here. Who is calling please?
Dan: It's Dan speaking.
Sukjai: Please call again tomorrow. Today Mr. Somchai is not coming back to the office.
Dan: Is that right? Thank you very much.

Conversation 2

Siri: Hi. Siri speaking.
Sue: Hello! May I speak with Lek?
Siri: Just a moment, please. ... Lek is on another line.
Sue: O.K. I'll call again later.

Conversation 3

Piti: When you were a student, what subject did you like the best?
Ron: I liked science and math. And you?
Piti: I liked English, but I wasn't good at it. What kind of work do you do?
Ron: I'm a doctor. I'm working at a hospital in America. And where do you work?
Piti.   I work with a French company.
Ron: Do you like your work?

Piti: Yes. My work requires a lot of foreign language skills. I get a chance to use what I've learned. Do you like being a doctor?

Ron: I don't like it so much. Although the money is good, I have to work very hard. I don't have very much time with my family.

Conversation 4

Sopon: Randy, how long have you been working here?
Randy: About three years. And you?
Sopon: I just started the beginning of this year.
Randy: You work very hard, don't you?
Sopon: I'm saving money to buy a house. Then I think I will get married.
Randy: Do you already have a girlfriend?
Sopon: Yes. Here name is Oi. She is two years younger than I. I was born in the Year of the Rabbit. Oi was born in the Year of the Snake.
Randy: I wish you good luck.

Test
Answers

Test Answers

Test 1 (page 25)

Matching:

1. h   2. p   3. 1   4. q   5. i   6. k   7. b   8. j
9. m   10. g   11. n   12. d   13. f   14. c   15. o

Translation:

1. The school is that way.
2. I don't like the hot season.
3. The weather is good today.
4. That person comes from the South.
5. I will go to Khon Kaen next week.

Test 2 (page 41)

Matching:

1. q   2. k   3. n   4. r   5. 1   6. a   7. e   8. o
9. g   10. i   11. j   12. h   13. m   14. d   15. p

Translation:

1. When will you arrive in Thailand?
   -Three p.m.
2. Where will you stay?
   -At the Maenam Hotel
3. Where are you going?
   -I will go shopping.
4. Where is the police station?
   -Turn left, then go straight.
5. Where do you want to take a trip to?
   -I want to go to Lumpini Park.

Test 3 (page 54)

Matching:

1. g   2. r   3. a   4. l   5. h   6. p   7. q   8. m
9. n   10. f   11. i   12. j   13. k   14. o   15. c

Translation:

1. I don't want you to know.
2. Make Thai food for me (please).
3. Today we open for service at noon.
4. I want to borrow money from you.
5. Teachers give knowledge to students.

Test 4 (page 68)

Matching:

1. r   2. n   3. f   4. l   5. h   6. k   7. q   8. d
9. b   10. g   11. p   12. c   13. e   14. i   15. a

Translation:

1. He doesn't have education.
2. You should study Japanese.
3. We must have effort.
4. I am the manager of a Thai restaurant.
5. What places are you going to?

Test 5 (page 82)

Matching:

1. b   2. l   3. m   4. h   5. c   6. j   7. d   8. o
9. e   10. n   11. g   12. f   13. p   14. i   15. a

Translation:

1. He asked what your name is.
2. There is no storage space in my house.
3. We are beaten by the teacher.
4. Don't go there by yourself.
5. What do you call this in English?

Test 6 (page 101)

Matching:

1. b   2. a   3. c   4. q   5. r   6. j   7. p   8. k
9. o   10. h   11. l   12. f   13. m   14. e   15. i

Translation:

1. Today is very boring.
2. He is forgetful.
3. Don't be absent-minded.
4. I like patient people.
5. He has a girlfriend who often complains.

Test 7 (page 119)

Matching:

1. e   2. o   3. q   4. a   5. l   6. f   7. c   8. g
9. d   10. n   11. j   12. h   13. p   14. b   15. k

Translation:

1. Where did you lose the book?
2. He laughs loudly.
3. Don't buy fake items.
4. He doesn't agree with me.
5. I forgot to go shopping.

Test 8 (page 139)

Matching:

1. c   2. r   3. o   4. m   5. g   6. p   7. l   8. a
9. f   10. h   11. n   12. q   13. k   14. j   15. i

Translation:

1. He has a nephew in Thailand.
2. John remarried. His new wife is Thai.
3. The groom is handsome. The bride is also beautiful.
4. I am Muslim.
5. I am his relative.

Test 9 (page 159)

Matching:

1. b 2. c 3. j 4. h 5. p 6. a 7. r 8. l
9. n 10. e 11. k 12. g 13. i 14. m 15. f

Translation:

1. Stay here and behave yourself.
2. Don't play hard to get.
3. You play tennis very well.
4. I want two round trip tickets.
5. Let's make Thai food.

Test 10 (page 177)

Matching:

1. n 2. i 3. o 4. j 5. c 6. g 7. k 8. q
9. m 10. e 11. l 12. b 13. r 14. d 15. h

Translation:

1. How long have you been working for this company?
   -About five and a half years.
2. Somchai goes to work only on Monday and Tuesday.
3. Which year was he born?
   -Year of the Goat.
4. I will return to Thailand the beginning of next year.
5. I am not good for you.

About the Author

Benjawan Poomsan Becker (เบญจวรรณ ภูมิแสน เบคเกอร์) was born in Bangkok and spent her childhood in Yasothon, a small province in Northeast Thailand. Her family is ethnic Laotian, so she grew up speaking both Thai and Lao. She graduated from Khon Kaen University in Thailand in 1990, with a B.A. in English. Benjawan gained extensive experience teaching Thai to foreigners while studying for her M.A. in sociology in Japan with the Japan-Thailand Trade Association and Berlitz Language Schools, and in the US with Thai temples, Stanford University and private students. In 1994 she married Craig Becker. They reside in Berkeley, California where she continues to write and publish books on the Thai and Lao languages. She also has a translation and interpretation business. Her books include "Thai for Beginners", "Thai for Intermediate Learners", "Thai for Advanced Readers", "Thai für Angfänger", "Taigo No Kiso", "Thai-English, English-Thai Dictionary for Non-Thai Speakers", "Lao-English, English-Lao Dictionary for Non-Lao Speakers", "Lao for Beginners" and "Improving Your Thai Pronunciation".

P A I B O O N

PUBLISHING

The Publisher for Southeast Asian Languages and Cultures

Paiboon Publishing was established in 1996 in Berkeley, California, USA. We also have an office in Bangkok, Thailand, the capital of the most popular destination in Southeast Asia.

Our mission is to produce and publish high quality, user-friendly language books, audio, DVDs, and other materials that help people to communicate and make new friends while traveling and living in this region of the world. Our products are sold in bookstores throughout Thailand, through on-line and phone orders from our office in the US and our distributors in Europe and Australia. Our full product line is available and can be ordered on-line through our website **www.paiboonpublishing.com**.

Every attempt is made to improve the quality of our products. Your comments and input are always welcome. Please send them to: **paiboonpublishing@gmail.com**

www.paiboonpublishing.com

U.S. Office
Paiboon Publishing
PMB 256
1442A Walnut Street
Berkeley, CA 94709 USA
Tel: 1-800-837-2979
Fax: 1-866-800-1840

Thailand Office
Paiboon Publishing
582 Amarinniwate Village 2
Nawamin 90, Bungkum
Bangkok 10230 THAILAND
Tel: 662-509-8632
Fax: 662-519-5437

Software Dictionary Series

Talking Thai-English-Thai Dictionary
for Windows PC *via INSTANT DOWNLOAD*

ENGLISH
อังกฤษ
ang-grìt

THAI
SCRIPT
ภาษาไทย
paa-săa-tai

THAI
SOUND
เสียงไทย
sĭiang-tai

Thai–English
English–Thai

TALKING
DICTIONARY
DOWNLOAD
With Classifiers And Tones
For English Speakers

Authors: Benjawan Poomsan Becker
and Chris Pirazzi ©2010

Paiboon Publishing's software dictionary has some truly exciting features, designed to help English speakers communicate in Thai whether or not you can read the Thai alphabet:

More than 42,000 bold entries and more than 53,000 translations.

* Click to hear any Thai word, spoken by a native Thai speaker
* Easy-to-read pronunciation guides
* Search-by-Sound™ (below right)
* Multiple pronunciation systems
* Useful Vocabulary
* Enlarge text to any size
* Detailed introduction to speaking and writing Thai
* Classifiers for 15,000 noun entries
* See any Thai word in real-world fonts (below left)
* Supports Windows XP, Vista, and 7
* Size: Requires about 100MB (0.1GB) of disk space
* Free lifetime upgrades via internet

ง่าย   Sign Font

ง่าย   Modern Font

ง่าย   Formal Script Font

ง่าย   Traditional Calligraphy Font

Available by Download $32.95 *(Subject to Change)*
Purchase and Download at
www.paiboonpublishing.com

Talking Thai-English-Thai Dictionary Software Dictionary for Windows PC *via CD-ROM*

Our ground-breaking Windows software is also available on CD-ROM for those who prefer a physical package.

- Same software and features as the download product
- Free lifetime upgrades via internet
- Includes helpful 76-page booklet on speaking and understanding Thai

Suggested Retail Price $39.95 *(Subject to Change)*
Copyright 2010
ISBN 9781887521987 Booklet and one CD-ROM

Talking Thai-English-Thai Dictionary *for Apple™ iPhone, iPad and iPod Touch*

Now Paiboon's software dictionary is at your fingertips anywhere you go with your iPhone, iPad, or iPod Touch. An indispensable tool whether you're on a plane or standing in a busy street market. Same useful vocabulary, Search-by-Sound™, and Thai language introduction as our Windows software, but on your mobile device. Download from the Apple iTunes App Store now!

- Same high-quality sounds for every Thai word
- Same large fonts; full-screen support on iPad
- Use even when not connected to the internet
- Requires about 100MB (0.1GB) of free space
- Requires OS version 3.0 or later
- Free lifetime upgrades via Apple iTunes® App Store.

Available at the Apple iTunes® App Store as
"Talking Thai-English-Thai Dictionary" $24.99 *(Subject to Change)*

Lao for Beginners
Second Edition

The most informative Lao language book for foreigners. Designed for either self-study or classroom use. It teaches all four language skills speaking, listening (when used in conjunction with the CDs), reading and writing. Offers clear, easy, step-by-step instruction, building on what has been previously learned. Three audio CDs follow along with lessons in the book.

Paperback 265 pages
Copyright 2009
ISBN 9781887521871 Book
ISBN 9781887521895 Book & CDs

Authors: Buasawan Simmala and Benjawan Poomsan Becker

Suggested Retail Price
Book– $15.00
Book & three CDs– $35.00

Vietnamese for Beginners
Second Edition

The most informative Vietnamese language book for foreigners. Designed for either self-study or classroom use. It teaches all four language skills speaking, listening (when used in conjunction with the audio CDs), reading and writing. Offers clear, easy, step-by-step instruction, building on what has been previously learned.

The three audio CDs included in the boxed set follow along with lessons in the book.

Paperback 292 pages
Copyright 2008
ISBN 9781887521840 Book
ISBN 9781887521864 Book & CDs

Author: Jake Catlett

Suggested Retail Price
Book– $15.00
Book & three CDs– $35.00

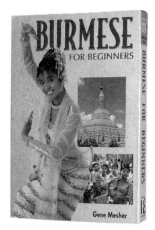

Burmese for Beginners

The perfect guide to mastering the Burmese language. Designed for either self-study or classroom use. It teaches all four language skills speaking, listening (when used in conjunction with the CDs), reading and writing. Offers clear, easy, step-by-step instruction, building on what has been previously learned. Three audio CDs follow along with lessons in the book.

Author: Gene Mesher

Suggested Retail Price
Book– $12.95
Book & three CDs– $32.95

Paperback 320 pages
Copyright 2006
ISBN 9781887521512 Book
ISBN 9781887521536 Book & CDs

Cambodian for Beginners
Second Edition

The best guide to learning beginning Khmer. Designed for either self-study or classroom use. It teaches all four language skills speaking, listening (in conjunction with the audio CDs), reading and writing. Offers clear, easy, step-by-step instruction, building on what has been previously learned.

The three audio CDs included in the boxed set follow along with lessons in the book.

Author: Richard K. Gilbert

Suggested Retail Price
Book– $15.00
Book & three CDs– $35.00

Paperback 300 pages
Copyright 2008
ISBN 9781887521819 Book
ISBN 9781887521833 Book & CDs

Thai for Beginners Series

The most popular book for learning basic Thai is now available as a book, software for your computer and as an Apple® iPhone App. Choose the best platform that works for you to make it most convenient to learn the Thai language.

Thai for Beginners
For Apple™ iPhone and iPad

Paiboon's new iPhone app makes is easy to study your Thai lessons wherever you go with your iPhone or iPod Touch. Similar to the PC software version but with the convenience of being able to review and do test exercises waiting for the bus, on a plane or on a park bench during your lunch break. The lessons follow the format of the *Thai for Beginners* book but a real Thai person speaks each of the over 3,000 words or phrases. Test your ability to hear and understand Thai or test your knowledge of written Thai with the built in exercises. Hearing the spoken Thai will help you increase the speed of learning the language that no book alone can do. Plus you'll find many new opportunities to practice your Thai since your iPhone will be with you all the time.

Authors: Benjawan Poomsan Becker and Dominique Mayrand

Copyright 2010

Available at the Apple iTunes® App Store As "Thai for Beginners" $24.99

Thai for Beginners
Book

One of the most popular books for learning basic Thai. Designed for either self-study or classroom use. It teaches all four language skills speaking, listening (when used in conjunction with the audio CDs), reading and writing. Offers clear, easy, step-by-step instruction, building on what has been previously learned. Used by many language schools in Thailand and Thai temples in the U.S. Two audio CDs follow along with lessons in the book. The book is an excellent companion to the iPhone app.

Paperback 262 pages
Copyright 1995
ISBN 9781887521000 Book
ISBN 9781887521161 Book & CDs

Author: Benjawan Poomsan Becker

Suggested Retail Price
Book– $12.95
Book & two CDs– $32.95

Thai for Beginners Software
for Windows PC computers

The best Thai language software available anywhere! Designed especially for Thai written script to help you to rapidly improve your listening and reading skills. Over 3,000 recordings of both male and female voices. The content is similar to the book *Thai for Beginners* but with interactive exercises and additional useful words and phrases. Select from multiple easy-to-read font styles and sizes. Super- crisp enhanced text with the Paiboon transliteration system which can be turned on or off for all items. Compatible with Microsoft Windows operating systems XP, Vista (32 bit) and 7 (32 bit).

Authors: Benjawan Poomsan Becker and Dominique Mayrand

Booklet 50 pages & one CD-ROM
Copyright 2003
ISBN 9781887521413 Book & CD-ROM

Suggested Retail Price
Booklet & one CD-ROM– $40.00

Thai Hit Songs Vol. 1
Music Video/DVD and Booklet

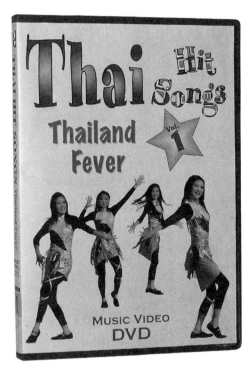

Author: Various Thai Artists

This DVD contains nine music videos from the Thai Hit Songs Vol. 1 music album. It features exciting performances of talented young Thai dancers, colorful illustrations, and beautiful scenes of Thailand that depict each song. You will be entertained by this fun music video and learn the Thai language at the same time. The booklet contains all the song lyrics with detailed explanations, song synopsis and translations. The songs are entertaining with catchy tunes and witty play-on-word lyrics in the pop song style that are new and refreshing to dance and sing to. Each song teaches a specific aspect of the Thai language as well. An excellent resource for Thai learners of all levels and a must have for lovers of Thailand and the Thai language. Kids love our music videos.

Booklet 96 pages & one DVD
Copyright 2010
Suggested Retail Price - $15.00
ISBN 9781887521338

Thai Hit Songs Vol. 1
Music CD and Booklet

Thai Hit Songs Vol. 1 is a unique innovative program to help you learn the Thai language as never before. It can be used alone or as a supplementary tool to our other Thai language learning materials. The music on the CD will get you excited and motivated to learn the Thai language. The booklet contains all the song lyrics with detailed explanations, song synopsis and translation. The songs are entertaining with catchy tunes and witty play-on-word lyrics in the pop song style that are new and refreshing to dance and sing to. Each song teaches a specific aspect of the Thai language as well.

Also available as downloads from the Apple iTunes store – without booklet

Author: Various Thai Artists

Booklet 96 pages & one Audio CD
Copyright 2010
ISBN 9781887521024

Suggested Retail Price
Booklet & one CD- $15.00

Improving Your
Thai Pronunciation

Designed to help foreigners maximize their potential in pronouncing Thai words and enhance their Thai listening and speaking skills. Students will find that they have more confidence in speaking the language and can make themselves understood better. The booklet and the audio CD are made to be used in combination. The course is straight forward, easy to follow and compact.

Author: Benjawan Poomsan Becker

Booklet 50 pages & one Audio CD
Copyright 2003
ISBN 9781887521260

Suggested Retail Price
Booklet & one CD - $15.00

Printed Dictionary Series

The best series of Thai, Lao and Burmese printed dictionaries available today! The new three-way look up system used in these dictionaries provides the easiest and most effective way to find the words you need.

Thai–English Dictionary

This practical and handy pocket size dictionary is designed to help English speakers communicate in Thai unlike any other Thai-English dictionary available today. Words can be looked up in English, by Thai script or by Thai sound making it easier to find the word you need. No other Thai-English dictionary provides the Paiboon transliteration system, which makes this dictionary an excellent companion to Paiboon's other Thai language books. Includes classifiers and tones and an extensive vocabulary of all the words you will use in everyday life including basic medical, cultural, political and scientific terms. The three sections include: Section One (Look up English), Section Two (Look up Thai script), and Section Three (Look up Thai sound).

Authors: Benjawan Poomsan Becker and Chris Pirazzi

Paperback - pocket size 4"x 5.5"
Copyright 2009
ISBN 9781887521321 Book
Suggested Retail Price Book $18.00

Burmese–English Dictionary

This concise and helpful pocket size dictionary has been designed to specifically aid English speakers to communicate effectively in Burmese. Words can easily be found by using one of the three sections. Section One (English-Phonetic-Burmese), Section Two (Burmese-Phonetic-English), and Section Three (Phonetic-Burmese-English). Words can be looked up in English, the Burmese script or the phonetic Burmese sound, whichever way is easier for you. Contains current up to date vocabulary and standard words specific to Burmese culture. An excellent resource and companion to Paiboon's *Burmese for Beginners*.

Paperback - pocket size 4"x 5.5"
Copyright 2009
ISBN 9781887521581
Suggested Retail Price Book $18.00

Authors: Aung Soe Min and
Nance Cunningham

Lao–English Dictionary

This functional and useful pocket size dictionary was created to assist English speakers to communicate successfully in Lao. Most Lao-English dictionaries either use only the Lao script or phonetic transliteration, making it difficult for English speakers to look up words. This revolutionary dictionary solves these problems by providing entries in three separate sections: Section One (English-Phonetic-Lao), Section Two (Phonetic-Lao-English), and Section Three (Lao-Phonetic-English). Using Paiboon's transliteration system, this dictionary is an excellent companion to Paiboon's *Lao for Beginners*. Includes tones and an extensive vocabulary for practically every situation including basic medical, scientific, political, and cultural terms.

Paperback - pocket size 4"x 5.5"
Copyright 2002
ISBN 9781887521277 Book
Suggested Retail Price Book $15.00

Authors: Benjawan Poomsan Becker and
Khamphan Mingbuapha

Author: Benjawan Poomsan Becker

Suggested Retail Price
Book– $12.95
Book & two CDs– $27.95

Thai for Intermediate Learners

The continuation of *Thai for Beginners*. Users are expected to be able to read and understand basic Thai language. There is a transliteration provided where new words are introduced. Two audio CDs follow along with lessons in the book.

Paperback 220 pages
Copyright 1998
ISBN 9781887521017 Book
ISBN 9781887521451 Book & CDs

Author: Benjawan Poomsan Becker

Suggested Retail Price
Book– $12.95
Book & two CDs– $27.95

Thai for Advanced Readers

The book introduces readers to various writing styles and offers a bridge to advanced reading and writing of the Thai language. Challenges readers to read Thai and keeps their attention with interesting cultural facts about Thailand. Also helps readers expand their Thai vocabulary in a systematic way. Two audio CDs follow along with lessons in the book.

Paperback 210 pages
Copyright 2000
ISBN 9781887521031 Book
ISBN 9781887521598 Book & CDs

Practical Thai Conversation DVD Volume 1

This exciting method for learning Thai comes with a booklet and a DVD that contains ten scenes of realistic conversations. You will enjoy watching and listening to this program and learn the Thai language at the same time. Greetings and introductions, asking directions, shopping, on the telephone and more conversations are included. Great for studying with your TV, desktop computer or laptop. A must for all Thai learners.

Author: Benjawan Poomsan Becker

Booklet 65 pages & one DVD
Copyright 2005
ISBN 9781887521475 Booklet & DVD

Suggested Retail Price
Booklet and DVD– $15.00

Practical Thai Conversation DVD Volume 2

Designed for intermediate Thai learners, it comes with a booklet and DVD that contains nine scenes of common and useful conversations. At the bank, looking for a place to rent, going to the Songkran festival and more. Can be played on your TV for computer. The course is straight forward, easy to follow and fun.

Author: Benjawan Poomsan Becker

Booklet 52 pages & one DVD
Copyright 2006
ISBN 9781887521642 Booklet & DVD

Suggested Retail Price
Booklet and DVD– $15.00

Speak like a Thai

www.speaklikeathai.com

The Thai language series you have been waiting for! You will be delighted to be able to express yourself in Thai. Key words and phrases in all volumes of this series are chosen from many spoken or written sources. The accompanying audio CD helps you learn and remember quickly. These words and phrases are not normally taught in standard Thai textbooks.

Suggested Retail Price Per Volume $15.00

Volume 1: Contemporary Thai Expressions

This program prepares you to communicate in real life situations. There are 500 entries in the booklet and audio CD. The key words and phrases are carefully chosen from many sources where they are spoken or written by Thai people. Expand your vocabulary with words and phrases that Thai people use all the time.

ISBN 9781887521390 Booklet & audio CD

Volume 2: Thai Slang and Idioms

The best collection of Thai slang words you will ever find. 250 entries are recorded on the audio CD and explained in the booklet with a brief translation, a literal translation and used in a sample phrase or sentence. Includes hundreds of sassy bonus words (not recorded) that you should only use with close friends.

ISBN 9781887521734 Booklet & audio CD

Volume 3: Thai Proverbs and Sayings

This booklet lists 400 common Thai proverbs and sayings that are often used by Thai people. Each entry has an English translation, a transliteration, the phrase written in Thai and a literal translation. Familiarize yourself by listening to the audio CD, then sprinkle them into your conversations. Your Thai friends will get a *kick* out of what they hear.

ISBN 9781887521741 Booklet & audio CD

Volume 4: "Heart" Words

Jai, which means 'heart' and also 'mind', is an important word in the Thai language. It is a special concept in the Thai culture and is included in many descriptive Thai words. You can increase your vocabulary manifold by combining the word *'jai'* with other words and phrases. Listen and learn how Thai people express their feelings and thoughts.

ISBN: 9781887521765 Booklet & audio CD

Volume 5: Northeastern Dialect

Wherever you go in Thailand, you will meet people from the Northeast (Isaan). The number of people from the Issan region comprises more than one third of the entire country's population. Many Isaan words are different from standard Thai: the Isaan dialect is almost the same as the Lao language. Once you learn this dialect, you will be able to use it in Laos as well.

ISBN: 9781887521772 Booklet & audio CD

Volume 6: Real Life Conversation

This volume contains 20 conversations of native Thai speakers in different situations ranging from greetings, visiting a friend's house to talking about politics. They are presented first at the normal speed of an actual conversation. Then each phrase is spoken with an English translation so you can repeat and familiarize yourself to the way Thai speakers express themselves.

ISBN: 9781887521963 Booklet & audio CD

Volume 7: Thai Abbreviations and Formal Thai

Learn hundreds of common Thai abbreviations. This audio CD contains 150 abbreviations with the corresponding Thai words and their English translation plus, 100 phrases of formal Thai with English translations with their colloquial versions. Bonus abbreviations are also provided in the appendix. Good for intermediate and advanced students.

ISBN: 9781887521970 Booklet & audio CD

Authors: Sunisa Terlecky and Philip Bryce

Suggested Retail Price
Book $19.95

Retiring in Thailand
Live in Paradise for Pennies on the Dollar

A very useful guide for those who are interested in retiring in Thailand. It contains critical information for retirees: how to get a retirement visa, banking, health care, renting property, making friends, everyday life issues, tips from expats living in Thailand and other important retirement factors. It also lists Thailand's top retirement locations. It's a must for anyone considering living the good life in the Land of Smiles.

Paperback 270 pages
Copyright 2007 – Second Edition
ISBN 9781887521796 Book
www.retiringinthailand.com

How to Buy Land and Build a House in Thailand

This book contains essential information for anyone contemplating buying or leasing land and building a house in Thailand. Subjects covered: land ownership options, land titles, taxes, permits, lawyers, architects and builders. Also includes English/Thai building words and phrases and common Thai building techniques. Learn how to build your dream house in Thailand that is well made, structurally sound and nicely finished.

Paperback 259 pages
Copyright 2007
ISBN 9781887521710 Book
www.retiringinthailand.com

Author: Philip Bryce

Suggested Retail Price
Book $19.95

Thai Law for Foreigners
The Thai Legal System Easily Explained

Written in plain language for common people to understand in both English and Thai, *Thai Law for Foreigners* introduces you to the history and development of Thai law, the structure of Thai government and the Thai court system. Explains legal procedures in Thailand for both criminal and civil matters, how to choose a lawyer, Thai lawyer's ethics and how to work with lawyers and interpreters.

Thai Law for Foreigners answers questions pertaining to family and personal matters including the requirements of Thai citizenship, engagement and dowry, prenuptial agreements, traditional wedding ceremonies, making a will, and divorce procedures. Gives information on living in Thailand such as renting a house, working with Thai employees, knowing your rights if you are arrested, things to be aware of and much more. Contains lots of useful information in the reference section and a glossary of the English and Thai legal terms used in the book.

This book will help you save time, money and the frustration of doing research to find out what you need to know about Thai law.

For further information and to view the table of contents, select sample pages and reference forms included in this book, please visit our website at: www.thailawforforeigners.com

Paperback 470 pages
Copyright 2008
Suggested Retail Price $21.95
ISBN 9781887521574 Book

Authors: Chris Pirazzi and
Vitida Vasant

Suggested Retail Price
Book– $15.95

Thailand Fever

Thailand Fever is the must-have relationship guidebook for Thais and foreigners. Written in both Thai and English, it lets each of you finally express complex issues by just pointing across the page. Thoughtfully designed... light and fun... very highly recommended. Before you start a relationship, find out what you are in for. The book is good even for people who have lived in Thailand and have been in a relationship with a Thai partner for a long time.

Paperback 258 pages
Copyright 2004
ISBN 9781887521482 Book
www.thailandfever.com

Author: Benjawan Poomsan Becker

Suggested Retail Price
Booklet & one CD– $15.00

Thai for Travelers

Thai for Travelers is your handy travel companion in the Land of Smiles. It contains hundreds of useful words and phrases for many situations. This book is especially designed for travelers with up-to-date and practical phrases that can be used instantly. The audio CD that accompanies the book will help you improve your pronunciation and expedite your Thai language learning. You can use it conveniently without having knowledge of the Thai language.

Booklet 95 pages and one CD
Copyright 2008
ISBN 9781887521789 Book & CD